T0131350

DADS UNDER CONSTRUCTION

DADS UNDER CONSTRUCTION

Adventures in Fatherhood

Neil R. Campbell, Ph. D.

THE DUNDURN GROUP
TORONTO · OXFORD

Copyright © Neil R. Campbell, 2003

All rights reserved. No part of this publication may be reproduced, stored in a retrieval system, or transmittedin any form or by any means, electronic, mechanical, photocopying, recording, or otherwise (except for briefpassages for purposes of review) without the prior permission of Dundurn Press. Permission to photocopyshould be requested from Access Copyright.

Copy-editor: Michael Hodge
Design: Jennifer Scott
Printer: Webcom

National Library of Canada Cataloguing in Publication

Campbell, Neil Robert
       Dads under construction : adventures in fatherhood / Neil Campbell.

ISBN 1-55002-472-8

1. Fatherhood. 2. Parenting. 3. Campbell, Neil Robert. I. Title.

HQ756.C34 2003   306.874'2   C2003-

1   2   3   4   5   07   06   05   04   03

 Conseil des Arts du Canada   Canada Council for the Arts Canadä  ONTARIO ARTS COUNCIL CONSEIL DES ARTS DE L'ONTARIO an Ontario government agency un organisme du gouvernement de l'Ontario

We acknowledge the support of the **Canada Council for the Arts** and the **Ontario Arts Council** for our publishing program. We also acknowledge the financial support of the **Government of Ontario**, through the **Ontario Book Publishing Tax Credit** and the **Ontario Media Development Corporation**, and the **Government of Canada**.

Care has been taken to trace the ownership of copyright material used in this book. The author and the pub-lisher welcome any information enabling them to rectify any references or credit in subsequent editions.

J. Kirk Howard, President

Dads Under Construction, Dads Can, and Dad Classes are registered trademarks of Neil R. Campbell.
www.dadscan.ca
1-888-DADS CAN (323-7226)

Dundurn
3 Church Street, Suite 500
Toronto, Ontario, Canada
M5E 1M2

In memory of my father,
Thomas Benjamin,
and for my daughters,
Ailène and Alexandra,
with love.

CONTENTS

ACKNOWLEDGEMENTS

This is a book of living memories — snapshots of my journey into fatherhood. The reader is invited, through reading about my experiences with my father and later with my own children, to understand how a man sees himself as "father."

In the Dad Class program that I facilitate at St. Joseph's Health Centre in London, Ontario, more than twelve hundred expectant and new fathers have been encouraged to construct for themselves a model of involved, responsible fathering. They have come to understand themselves as fathers, something that is so important to families and society today. A resource referred to in these classes is Dads Can, a national charitable organization founded in 1997, that promotes this model of involved fathering through various educational materials and programs.

This book would not be able to exist without the interactions that I have had with others, both recently and throughout my life. I particularly thank my mother Elma, who always encouraged and supported my father in his involvement with my sisters and me. My older sister Jeanette, before her death at such a young age, encouraged his increasing involvement with my younger sister Jean and myself. Jean challenged my father to grow with the changes that she experienced.

I thank my wife, Karen, for likewise encouraging and supporting my relationship with our daughters, Ailène and Alexandra, and for letting me find my own fathering style.

Dr. H. Aufreiter, Dr. E. Hanna, Dr. J. Lohrenz, and Dr. P. Steinberg assisted in opening numerous doors for me and encouraged my self-examination. I am in their debt. Dr. Beth Mitchell, psychologist, provided her expertise in child development to this book. I thank her for that.

The experiences of all those dads who have participated in the Dad Class over the years highlighted for me the various paths that fathers take in their journeys. To all of them I express my appreciation.

Donald G. Bastian had the foresight to support this book project from the start. I cannot thank him enough for his superb editing and book publishing skills.

Dr. Diane Whitney arrived on the scene at an important time and quickly demonstrated support for this book. Thank you.

I also thank St. Joseph's Health Centre and the London Health Sciences Centre for their ongoing support of Dads Can and its programs.

My secretaries Lynda Cowie, Debra Roche, and Janice Seaborn were very patient with my typing requests.

The Lawson Foundation, The Walter J. Blackburn Foundation, and the board members of Dads Can have always been behind this project. Thank you, as well.

And of course, my deepest thanks to my father and my daughters, who taught me how to be a dad. I love you very much.

FREEZING MY FATHER'S PYJAMAS

I was fifteen years old, the time of life when mischief takes hold of a young man. Who better a target than my father, who was a staid fifty-eight? He was an industrious man who worked long hours operating a laundromat and working as a telegrapher with the railway. Out of necessity, he usually went to bed early.

My father had a thing about being cold. He often felt chilly. Winter was never his favourite season. And of course, his creature comforts at bedtime were very important to him. He always had his pyjamas folded neatly under his pillow, and he looked forward to getting into a warm bed for a good night's sleep.

One evening, several hours before his bedtime, I snuck into the master bedroom and took his pyjamas from under his pillow. I quietly made my way to the laundry room, filled my mother's laundry spray bottle with cold water, and sprayed the PJs thoroughly. Then I put them into the freezer. One hour later, shortly before he went upstairs to get ready for bed, I retrieved the pyjamas, which by then were frozen stiff, and put them back under his pillow. I left the room and waited in gleeful anticipation as he came upstairs and prepared to go to bed.

From down the hallway came his startled exclamation. He immediately called out to my mother, wanting to know who was responsible for this deed. He got to bed somewhat later than usual that night because he had to defrost the pyjamas in the dryer.

I played this trick on him several times during my teen years, and he would always give the same startled yelp. He knew very well who was freezing his pyjamas. Years later, he told my mother that he appreciated this prank I'd played on him. He said that in a strange sort of way, it made him feel important.

During the period when I was growing up, in the 1950s and 60s, "father" meant the authority figure, the one in charge, the breadwinner. Certain roles were expected of my father, even though he did not always understand how to play them out in his own life. He resolved this uncertainty by working very hard, the only thing he knew how to do, and the only thing he was sure was expected of men. The frozen pyjamas prank I pulled on my father was one way I had of poking fun at him — a way to challenge his authority role. I had found a way to engage him in play.

As the years passed, my father grew wise enough to see this. Instinctively, he knew it was because I cared so deeply about him, and because I cared about what he thought of me, that he had become the target of this and other pranks. That's what he had meant when he told my mother that it made him feel important. He sensed that this was one way I had of differentiating myself from him, of declaring my own personhood, separate and distinct from him. At the same time, it was a way that we could connect with each other. That's why he never really became angry about the frozen pyjamas.

Some children find it difficult to find positive ways to declare their independence. They may resort to negative "acting out" behaviour, such as getting into trouble at school or perhaps breaking curfew. So, too, some fathers find it difficult to let go of the authority role. They cannot bear to have this role challenged. Sometimes they absent themselves from the situation altogether. When that dynamic emerges, the scene is set for a power struggle that can reverberate throughout a child's life, right into adulthood. My father received the message from my pranks that I needed to challenge his role, and he accepted this playfully. He and I grew closer in our relationship.

PIG TIED TO A WAGON

My father shared very few stories with me of his own childhood, and what he did share was usually at my prompting. My father was raised on a one hundred and fifty acre farm located ten kilometres north of Elmira, Ontario. Farming in the area was mixed, but focussed on growing a variety of seed grains. My father's was a self-sufficient farm typical of the time: crops included hay, vegetables, and a variety of fruits, while the livestock consisted of cattle, horses, pigs, and chickens.

It was difficult for me to comprehend my father simply having fun as a child.

One playful story he recalled was in the context of hard work. Two other stories were of mishaps that were quite painful to him, and one of them made him feel devalued by a family member.

With these three stories that he would tell me, it was always left up to me to determine what the meaning of them had been for him.

The playful story was of an incident when he was nine years of age and playing with his older brother with a children's wagon in the farmyard behind the barn. After awhile, they became bored and decided to liven things up a bit. They went into the pigpen and tied a pig to the front of the wagon. Both my uncle and my father attempted to sit down inside the wagon with the intention that the pig would pull them. Just as they got inside the wagon though, the pig started running all over the pen. Suddenly the wagon tipped over and both my uncle and my father fell out. The pig then continued running toward the fence. The wagon shattered as it hit the railings. The fence itself toppled and the pig ran off, dragging the rope and pieces of wood behind it. My uncle and father scrambled to their feet and started chasing after the pig. Eventually they were able to corner it and bring it back to the pen.

When they got back, my grandfather was standing there looking very stern indeed. He scolded them for the damage that had been done and told them to fix the fence. And he announced that they would not get a new wagon.

To me, it sounded like an ingenious, playful activity for my father to engage in, like something fun with a disastrous outcome. My father did not see it that way.

In the second story that he would tell me, he was about eleven years old. Working in the barn, he cornered a squirrel, bent down, and tried to pick it up. The squirrel, quite frightened, bit my father's thumb, piercing his nail. The injury was incredibly painful, and he had to be seen by the local doctor. He received several stitches to his thumb and was left with scars for the rest of his life.

In the third story, my father recalled a time that he was visiting relatives. He had not yet entered puberty and was still quite short for his age. His cousin, who was the same age, had grown considerably the previous year. Immediately upon entering his relatives' home, my father was asked by his aunt to stand beside his suddenly lanky cousin. Comparisons of their height were made, and his aunt pointed out the disparity in size to the family members present. My father felt quite devalued by this situation and by his aunt, and the feeling would stay with him all of his life.

Most of the time my father was an all-work-and-no-play sort of guy. I figured out pretty early in my life that if I wanted to play with my father, I would have to teach him how. To hear a story about a pig tied to a wagon helped me to understand that at one time my father had been a boy and had known how to have fun.

The scar on his thumb always reminded me that my father had had a childhood. I knew he had been a typical boy who took risks — in his case wanting a pet and ending up with an injury. I was also reminded by his memory of the comparison that his aunt made between him and his cousin and how it made him feel. Sometimes I felt put-down in this way in situations with others. Being able to reflect on my father's experience helped me realize that I was not alone.

My father was such a hard worker that it was difficult for me to imagine that he was once a little boy who could have fun. These three stories he often told me allowed me to identify with him whether I was having fun, getting injured, or feeling self-conscious — three states of being that pretty well sum up being a boy.

Telling children our stories, and even those of our fathers, is of great importance. We dads often forget, as we deal with our children, that we, too, were once kids who liked to have fun and who grew up. The journey from boyhood to manhood to fatherhood, in particular, is an important path. Through telling them the stories of our own childhoods, we provide our children with a sense of awareness that something has gone on before them and that something will follow. Children are then able to feel, in effect, that they are a part of history.

GENERATIONS

When my uncle died, my father gave me a large box of family photographs, but I was not able to find any pictures of his father. My grandfather died a number of years before I was born, when my father was a teenager. I have searched a number of sources and have spoken to neighbours who lived near the home where my father grew up. Same result: no photos.

My grandfather's death was sudden. He had a heart attack on the front lawn of the family home early one morning as he and his sons went out to do the usual chores on the farm.

My grandfather, and previous generations on my father's side of my family, are known to me only in the stories my father told me. I have always found these stories fascinating. Several years prior to my father's death, he started looking into his family tree and documenting his history. Fortunately, he was able to research back several generations.

It was different on my mother's side of the family. I knew her father very well. He was a cabinetmaker who had a carpentry shop behind his home in Kitchener, Ontario. My grandfather was the son of a German immigrant who was a shoemaker. Skilled tradesmen abounded in my mother's family. They also had a strong German heritage, something of which my grandfather was particularly proud. I remember him speaking and reading in German, and the meals I ate in his home, and in my own, were very traditional. I marvelled at how Grandpa made his own sauerkraut and allowed us to eat it right out of the fermenting barrel located in his basement.

As a child, I would often visit him, and looked forward to playing beside him as he worked. The equipment and the tools in his shop enthralled me. I remember the smell of the wood and the sound of the motors as he made various pieces of furniture. I recall him as a stern yet friendly man with an unusual sense of humour. My sisters and I would frequently go to visit him in his shop while he worked.

When we entered his home, he would always have a dish of candies on a table just for us. Along with making furniture, he also made various games that we children could play.

Fortunately, my mother's brother kept an extensive family history and a very informative family tree that went back quite a number of generations. Like my father's stories, this history provided me with a sense of previous generations. As I entered my teen years, my grandfather died. However, he left me with many fond memories.

What I have learned from my grandfathers and their histories is how hard they had to work and how difficult the times had been for them. "Back then," hard work was the order of the day, whether it was within or outside of the family, both for parents and for children. My mother was often called on to take care of her brothers, sister, and parents.

After they were married, my mother and father followed the models of their parents. My father focussed on working outside the family, while my mother was deeply involved within the family. However, once my sisters and I were attending public school on a full-time basis, my mother and father opened a laundry business and their roles, to some degree, reversed. My mother worked increasingly outside the home in the laundry business. My father was now busier in his work, adding the laundry work to his railway work, yet he began to participate more actively in family life. This was not easy for him.

Children often feel that the world began at their birth. Learning their family history helps them see that their parents were once children, and that they, too, will grow up and become adults. A sense of history gives them a feeling of responsibility, not just to their own families, but to the past as well.

Through my father and mother telling me their histories, and my being able to connect with these, I have come to realize that I am not alone as I father the next generation. This awareness brings with it integrity.

Knowing my father's history has helped me to make adjustments to my work and home lives, in particular guarding me from the perils of overworking. In the past it was necessary to work hard, with little if any leisure time. Today, as hard as work still is, society has the luxury of increased recreational time. It has not always been easy for me to keep a balance between work, play, and family. I feel it is important to model the need for such balance for my own children. Through my father telling me his history and providing me with the opportunity to understand it, I have been given a sense of choice. I don't just work, I choose to work. I am also aware of the need to relax and enjoy life.

A father telling his story to his child provides the child with a sense of genealogical awareness, along with choice. This choice is how the child can continue living part of the family history while creating a new history at the same time.

MOVING TOO FAST

My father worked as a telegrapher for the Canadian National Railway for approximately forty-five years. The railroad was the cord that tied him to his family and yet let him move beyond that family to the outside world. The railroad was his ticket from rural life into city life.

My father loved the railroad, and he would often go for long walks along the tracks at the end of a work day. When I was old enough, probably about six, I would join him. It was a time when he and I could be alone together.

I can remember having trouble keeping up with him. The railway ties were perfectly spaced for me; I could walk on each one of them. For my father, they were too close together; he needed to take two at a time. This awkwardness of walking side by side often had me calling out for him to slow down. He would always do so, but shortly after we started out together again, the same problem would occur.

Walking along the railway tracks was not the only time this problem came about. I also often had to ask my father to slow down when I accompanied him to work, as we walked hand in hand on the sidewalk.

My father was a tall man with a long stride and large hands. He liked to move fast. I remember holding his hand as we walked along, marvelling at how large it was compared to mine. Sometimes I would try on his shoes. I could put one of my shoes right inside one of his. When I tried on his hat, it fell over my face. His winter coat was heavy enough to pull me to the ground when I put it on.

My father was also a strong man. From his childhood on the farm and on, he was used to working with his hands and lifting heavy objects. Any attempts on my part as a young boy to lift similar items would often be met with disaster.

Without a doubt my father was frustrated by my constant requests for him to slow down. He never exhibited this frustration, however, and patiently followed through on what I asked. But the problem would soon re-emerge.

Again I would have to ask him to slow down. Eventually, my father would pick me up in his arms. Problem solved.

It was not only moving fast that I was having problems with, it was also my father's size. When I looked up at him, he looked like a giant. I noticed the same reaction in each of my daughters when they were small and would put their hands in mine and marvel at the comparison in size. They too would put their shoes inside of mine and would constantly say how big I was.

When we adults look down at a child, we tower over them. It is beneficial to children for us to bend down when talking to them, or to get down on one knee and face them eye-to-eye.

Your child views you as a strong person, a hero. Your responsibility as a father is to meet your child at his or her level and to follow the pace they set for you. Listen to what they need; they will tell you.

EXPLODING THE TULIPS

E arly every fall, my father carefully planted tulip bulbs in the garden that bordered the outside walls of our home. He enjoyed this task, and always looked forward to his gardening. He spent a great deal of time designing the correct layout of the bulbs that he wanted and then planting them. The following spring, in May, they would bloom in a lovely pattern of colours. It was a beautiful sight. As they bloomed, he would gingerly tend to them, preparing the soil around their bases and pulling out any weeds that may have started to grow.

Also in May is the national holiday marking Queen Victoria's birthday, when it is traditional to light firecrackers through the preceding weekend and on Victoria Day itself. My mother was quite hesitant about my lighting any firecrackers when I was young. However, she did find very small ones that I could light. We called them "ladyfingers." My mother would start a piece of string smouldering and send me outside with it. I would light each of the firecrackers with this piece of string. As I gained confidence in lighting them and my mother felt that I was practicing care, she would leave me alone outside. I devised all sorts of activities with these firecrackers.

One of these times when I was outside lighting firecrackers, my father was grooming the tulips at the front of the house. They were growing quite well, and the large colourful blossoms looked very healthy. He slowly worked his way around the front of the home to the side and then around the corner to the back. As he disappeared from sight, I suddenly had an impulse to place one of the ladyfingers in one of the tulip heads. I lit it. It was quite satisfying how the entire tulip head exploded and the petals shot up into the air and floated slowly to the ground. I gathered the petals and put them in my pocket. I decided to go onto the next tulip head and do the same. I continued to do this along the front row of the house. Performing this deed efficiently from tulip to tulip gave me a great sense of accomplishment.

Eventually my father came back around to the front of the house to start watering the tulips. Kneeling to sprinkle water from a can around the stem of the tulip, he was shocked to see nothing there except stigma and stem. Looking down the row, he saw a number of other tulips in the same sad condition. At the same time, he watched me walk slowly around the corner of the house. I did not realize he had seen me, nor did it dawn on me that I was actually destroying his labour of love.

My father stood up and quickly ran toward the corner of the house. He took hold of my arm, took away the string and the firecrackers, and told me to come inside with him. He sat me down in one of the chairs in the kitchen and proceeded to tell me about the amount of work he had put in to growing and caring for these tulips. It was a scolding of sorts, but beyond being sent to my room for a time-out period, there was no further disciplinary action.

That fall, wise man that he was, my father made sure I was involved with him in the planning stage of where the next year's tulip bulbs would go. We also planted them together.

My father and I both learned a valuable lesson from this incident. As a boy, I was acting out my normal aggression, perhaps even aggression toward my father. It was something I needed to do. Meanwhile, my father was observing (and so was I) how he was handling his frustration over his tulips and his anger toward me. He did not try to cover up his true feelings of anger, but he found a way for us both to channel our feelings of anger through working together. In time I, too, would be a father facing similar issues with my children and would draw on this encounter to problem-solve each new one.

As important as it is for father and child to play and have fun together, there are also times when a child may act out. Quite often this is during the initial stages of (and throughout) adolescence, but it may happen at any time. In a sense, acting out is a way for a child to express individual-ity, sometimes assertively or even aggressively. What is important is the father's ability to handle that aggression and to help his child understand what is happening. A child watches how a father reacts very closely. Will the reaction be aggressive in kind or patient and understanding?

An involved father helps his child to modulate that aggression. My father's reaction taught me how to handle feelings of frustration and anger as I grew up. When my two daughters act out, I know that the most important thing is to help them understand their behaviour and the effects it has on all those involved.

A good example of this creative and constructive channelling of energies is how fathers and sons engage in hockey. Here is an opportunity for a father to teach his son how to be assertive, while at the same time exhibiting respect for other players as well as referees. However, there are fathers who respond to their sons' games aggressively, which sends all the wrong signals.

Throughout a child's formative years, a father who reacts constructively to acting out is teaching respect for others. By working out a consequence that fits the "crime," the child is better able to understand his or her behaviour.

LEARNING TO RIDE A BIKE

We had carefully practiced this on a number of occasions over the past several days. My father and I walked my new bicycle over to the parking lot behind the insurance company near our home. I was seven years old and quite eager, like many of my friends, to ride a bike on my own. I would stand on the curb and carefully climb up onto the bike as my father held it steady. My father would patiently walk beside me, holding the bike as I learned to balance and started to pedal. It became apparent that in a day or two it would be time for me to go solo. We both agreed on the day that I would try.

When the big day arrived, my father and I again walked over to the parking lot, and I climbed onto the bicycle. We started out side by side, he holding the handlebars and me beginning to push harder and harder on the pedals. He started to run beside me while holding the bike. Then he cried out that he would give me one last push. He did so while standing back and letting go of the handlebars. At first the front wheel wobbled and I was frightened. Then I heard my father call out, "Pedal harder; harder!" I did, and I felt the bike straighten out and surge forward. My father's voice began to fade. I was now biking on my own, and was quite proud of the achievement. I glanced back to look at my father and to show him how I was doing. That's when I noticed how far back he actually was. Carefully turning the bike around, I pedalled back to him.

As I got off the bike after coming to a clumsy stop, my father beamed with pride and gave me a hug.

I had not yet mastered the ability to get up on the bike and start out on my own; however, I would achieve this within the next several days. Eventually, I started to bike over to that parking lot without my father.

My father recognized at this stage in my life that learning how to ride a bike was an important part of my journey toward independence. I wanted to be like my friends who were all riding their bicycles. So he bought me a new bike, something he himself never had, and he spent a great deal of time just being patient as I learned to ride it. In each of those attempts to ride, I felt secure with my father holding me up. Then he realized the time had arrived to push and let me go.

My learning to ride a bicycle gave both of us a feeling of achievement. By being dependent on my father, I developed a sense of my own independence. By striking the right balance between holding onto me and letting me go, my father was being an excellent teacher and coach.

Your child's ever-developing independence is precisely based, in all situations, on your knowing when to support and when to let go. You need to be there. First you will take the lead, then you will be shoulder-to-shoulder, and then you will step back slowly, moving into the background. Both you and your child will learn when to hold each other and when to let go. And even when you separate, each of you carries a part of the other inside.

ROOFTOP ATTACK

I was eleven years of age and my younger sister Jean was nine. It was a lovely, sunny Saturday afternoon in the summer. My father had noticed for several weeks that the grouting on the chimney was in need of repair. He took the ladder out of the garage and climbed up onto the roof of our one-storey ranch-style home, taking with him several tools and a bucket of cement.

While he was working on the roof, I went around to the side of the house where the ladder was and quietly removed it. When he realized that he needed several more tools, he discovered the ladder was gone. He immediately called out for me and asked me if I had removed the ladder. I stated that I had and initiated a process of negotiation, my final offer being that if I were to let him off the roof, he would not discipline me. Eventually, an agreement was reached. I put the ladder back up, and my father came down. He obtained more materials and went back up on the roof.

By this time, my sister had come outside to play. She and I put our heads together and decided we would play a prank on him. Quietly, we removed the ladder from the side of the house. I went to the front door and locked it, and then my sister and I each went to opposite sides of the dwelling. On each of those sides was an outside water tap with a garden hose connected to it. We turned on the hoses and prepared ourselves.

Again, my father came over to the point where the ladder had been, and once again it was gone. A second time he called out for me. I responded by running around the side of the house with the garden hose and shooting a fine spray of water up at him on the roof. My father immediately backed up and decided it would be more to his advantage to go to the other side of the roof in order to get away from me. He climbed over the peak, only to discover that my sister was waiting for him. She sprayed him as well. My father was now in a predicament on the peak of the roof. He moved down toward the chimney and stayed there. Again, after another round of negotiations, a deal was struck that neither my sister nor I would be disciplined if we quit spraying him; we put the ladder up to the side of the roof and let him down.

My sister and I were not finished with him yet. We had discovered that both hoses could reach the point where my father would come down from the ladder. Jean came running around one corner and I came running around the other, each of us with hose in hand, catching our father in the crossfire. He made a mad dash toward the front door of the house, which of course I had locked. My father was now in a difficult situation, with my sister and me spraying water at him through the screen door. He started knocking on the door and ringing the doorbell, calling for my mother to let him in. She eventually opened the door and my father stumbled inside.

My mother immediately took charge of the situation and told my sister and me to stop. We retreated back to the side of the house, realizing there were going to be some consequences to our prank. Soon enough, my father came out and informed me that he was so wet he had to change. My mother accompanied him and asked us for a truce so he could finish his work. I do not recall my father ever being upset or disciplining us for this incident.

My father's family had taught him one value, and that was hard work. He grew up on a farm, with its constant round of daily chores. It was difficult for my father to break that habit and put down his work to involve himself with my sisters and me in fun. This was a language that he hadn't learned as a child. My father always seemed to be at his job as a telegrapher. He also worked in the evenings and weekends in the laundry that he and my mother had started. In what spare time was left, he did a great deal of house maintenance and gardening. I would frequently engage with my father in one of these activities as a way of being with him.

Our silly prank was an attempt to turn his work into some sort of fun, playful activity. Jean and I were both trying to find a moment with our father where we could be doing something together that from a child's perspective we enjoyed. In a way, the child was teaching the father how to play as much as the father was teaching the child how to work.

A number of years later, after my father's death, I was speaking to my mother about this incident. She told me that he quite often spoke about the moment and how it made him feel close to my sister and me. He told her that he found it difficult to know how to engage and play with us. When we came up with an idea like this one, he pretended not to be part of it, but he actually was. In a way, my father welcomed such occurrences between us. My father needed us, his children, to take the lead in this.

A child and a father often play-wrestle, roughhouse, and generally just enjoy physical engagement with one another. A child needs this connection to a father. A father does not just give a toy to his child; he is the toy. If a father is to be a toy, he needs to know how to play. My father learned how to play by observing and participating in what my sisters and I created out of our imaginations. It was our way of engaging him in a relationship with us. Little did we know that we were actually teaching him the value of play and of just having fun. We found a special way for all of us to be together.

DEATH OF A SISTER

One summer weekend, on the way to the cottage my family rented each year for a week, my older sister Jeanette, then sixteen, complained of not feeling well. The bright sunlight coming into the car was bothering her, she had several cankers in her mouth, and she felt quite tired. Jeanette had been feeling this way for several weeks now, and her condition was worsening. My parents had taken her to the family doctor on numerous occasions, but nothing could be diagnosed.

As a ten-year-old, I was excited, as were my two sisters, about going to the cottage. My excitement contributed to my not being aware of how Jeanette was feeling. For the entire week at the cottage, she found it very difficult to go out in the sunlight, as it bothered her eyes. She would often be found in her room with towels and blankets over the windows, feeling exhausted. My parents were at a loss as to what they should do.

Immediately upon our return home, my parents took Jeanette to the doctor. He consulted several other physicians and eventually diagnosed Jeanette with systemic lupus. At that time, in the early 1960s, there was limited, if any, treatment for lupus. My parents were informed that there was not much that could be done. It was only a matter of time before she would die.

My parents tried everything they possibly could. They even sent a physician to Europe to attend a conference on lupus, which had just recently been identified as an illness. However, he returned with no news on how to treat the condition.

Over the next several months, our family tried to live life normally. My sister became increasingly ill, and eventually she was unable to attend school. She was frequently at home in bed, often sleeping, and her classmates would bring her homework to her. By Christmas time, my sister was not able to leave her room, and the family would take turns sitting vigil with her. Sometimes several of us were together with her. My younger sister Jean and I were never really informed about our sister's actual condition. We believed that she would recover in time.

I remember that Christmas season well. Jeanette was unable to get out of bed to join in the festivities. Jean and I would often read her stories and visit her in her room in an attempt to cheer her up, but for the most part she would just lie there sleeping. On one rare occasion when Jeanette was well enough and felt energized, she and several of her friends went downtown and she had a picture taken of her, which she gave to my parents as a gift. Accompanying this photograph was a note expressing how much she loved them. She was obviously aware that her situation was serious.

In January, my sister was taken to the hospital for several visits. Later that month, I was home alone with her, sitting next to her bedside, when she screamed out in pain and went into convulsions. I was not sure what to do and tried to hold her in the bed until she calmed down. I called the family doctor who rushed over. I also called for an ambulance, and Jeanette was taken to the hospital. I never saw her again. She died several days later, in the early morning hours, with my father at her bedside.

My father drove home from the hospital and both he and my mother functioned as if nothing had happened. They felt that they should get everything in order before they told Jean and me. I recall my father driving both my sister and me to school and then, shortly thereafter, showing up to take us home again. Then they informed us of Jeanette's death.

Throughout the difficult time when my sister was at home ill, each evening my mother would go into the bathroom and cry. I remember standing in the hallway and hearing her, unsure of what was happening. My father withdrew, becoming silent and sullen. He did a great deal of outside work around the house, but he seemed to do it in isolation. Shortly after my sister died, a neighbour attempted to bring some flowers to the door, and my father burst out in anger at the neighbour and slammed the door in her face. My sister's bedroom remained untouched for several years, and my father made it clear that Jean and I were not to go in it.

My father was unable to acknowledge the fact that my sister had died. My mother at least expressed her grief, but my father held everything inside. Over time, my sister became idealized in the family. My father developed a depression that would remain with him for the rest of his life.

At the time of her death, Jeanette was seven years older than I was. For my father and mother, Jeanette blazed the trail for each of them to understand what it was to have a child who was going through adolescence. My father had to learn how to parent differently from what he had experienced as a child. He could not expect her to constantly be working like he had to. Jeanette became very close to my father's brother and mother and enjoyed visiting them on the farm. She had a special attachment with them and with my father.

The helplessness that my parents felt must have been terrible during those last six months, as my sister's illness worsened. My mother was able to vent it, though only to herself; my father, meanwhile, was not.

My father always told me that time goes by quickly and that children grow up fast. It was always difficult for me to understand this concept. However, now that I have my own children, and one of them has recently entered her teen years, I see how quickly time has gone by. It is important to live with your children, to be there and be involved in all levels of activity in their lives as they grow and change. Being a part of the lives of your children is a truly enriching experience. Watching them grow up is something that you will treasure forever. My father felt that time had slipped by too quickly in his relationship with Jeanette, and then it was gone.

Besides learning just how quickly time passes, I have come to see how important it is to keep channels of communication open and to express feelings with your child as much as is reasonably possible, being sensitive to what they can actually understand. Unfortunately, my father held everything in during this time, developing in the process an incredible level of frustration and anger. As he internalized this anger, he became depressed, bursting out in rage from time to time at the smallest infraction. I believe there were times that my father avoided talking about my sister because it was too difficult for him to deal with his feelings. What my father did not want to recall, he could not forget about. It would have helped him to have expressed some feelings, both inside and outside of the family. To share some of the situation within the family would have helped us all, but he understandably found this very difficult to do. In a strange way it was almost as if he was keeping a secret. For years afterwards, it was difficult for all of us in the family to reach a level of closure regarding my sister. It wasn't just because my father did not talk about it; it was also because none of us talked about it either.

Reflecting on my sister's death helps me understand what my father said about time passing by so quickly. A child's life in a family does go by very fast. They grow up and they move on. It is important to be there with your child, to be involved and to be responsible, and to enjoy the time together. Keeping your child up to date and expressing in a reasonable way how you are feeling permits communication channels to remain open. This is a very important learning experience for your child, as one day they will grow up and perhaps have a family of their own. They must learn the value of communication with their own children.

FATHER AS FRIEND

I t was late in the spring, and I was in my final term of grade nine. It had been a very difficult year for me, as I had to adjust to high school while at the same time finally reaching puberty. This was an event I was waiting for, yet feared. I was small in stature and still socially immature. Several of my grade nine classmates and some other teenagers in the high school frequently teased me. I felt quite insecure and unsure of myself, and my grades suffered that first year. It was a major adjustment for me to enter into a large new school and meet so many new people. At the start, I found it difficult to make friends; that, however, would slowly change.

For several years, my parents rented out a basement suite in our home to university students from out of town. During this particular year in grade nine, a first year student, Mike, was living in the basement. He was nineteen and attending his first year in an engineering degree program. It was his first time away from home, so he looked forward to receiving mail from his parents and girlfriend. In the evenings after supper I would often go downstairs to visit him. Sometimes I did my homework alongside him. We got along very well. He told me he had a younger brother my age, so it was easy for him to participate in activities that he knew I would enjoy. We went to hockey and basketball games together and attended the local sportsmen's show.

Mike was indeed like an older brother to me. My father frequently played catch with me and joined me in other activities, but he was much older than most of my friends' dads. At times it was difficult for him to keep up with my energy level. Mike was able to do this without any trouble.

April came, and it was the end of the university term for Mike. He finished writing his exams, packed up his car, and prepared to return home until the following September. I remember one evening standing on the hill at the side of the house, saying goodbye to him. As he backed his car out of the driveway, I started to cry. My father, who was working at the side of the house with a neighbour, noticed that I was distraught and came over and hugged me. He sensed the loss that I was experiencing and said, "I'll be your friend." With those words, I calmed down. Even though I realized that there were some things that Mike and I could do together that my father and I could not, my father was still there for me to turn to.

After that incident, my father made more attempts to participate in activities with me. Throughout the following summer, we did a great deal together. I spoke to him about how I felt about high school. He listened. By the time I entered grade ten, I felt more confident and better able to relate to my peers.

It was much easier for my father, given his all-work-and-no-play childhood, to follow the play as opposed to initiating it. However, though it was fun to join in activities with my father, as a child I welcomed someone else who could create other fun with me. Mike was able to teach me things that my father was not all that aware of or couldn't do, whether it was playing football, attending a magic show, or problem-solving the "new math."

Without a doubt, Mike's leaving was a real loss for me. However, my father's consistency and friendship remained behind. He had been able to identify my need for friendship with a male other than himself, but he had also realized that once this friend was gone, he as father needed to fill the vacuum.

The father–child relationship is similar to that of a dance in which each person moves toward, together, away, and independent of each other. It takes time and practice to understand and learn the dance. It can only be achieved by a father's attempts to understand himself and his history, and how he involves himself with the needs of his child, family, and partner. This dance, a closeness that in time leads to letting go, is at the heart of the friendship that develops between a father and his child.

PULLING AWAY

I was seventeen, and it was the summer prior to my first year in university. I had tuition to pay, so I had worked most of that summer in a grocery store. Since I needed as much working time as possible, I signed on for both day and night shifts. Needless to say, I was feeling very tired.

It was late on one of the night shifts, and I was putting up stock in the soap aisle. The large cases of soap boxes were extremely heavy and difficult to move around. While I was working, I glanced up and noticed a large inflatable cow — part of a display advertising milk — hanging from the ceiling. I thought this was an interesting item, one that would look wonderful hanging up in my room at home, so I decided to remove it.

It took some creative scheming to figure out how to get at it. I pulled a rather large skid full of soap boxes underneath the cow and gingerly climbed up on top. I removed my case cutter and, leaning over, attempted to cut the string that tied the back of the cow to the ceiling. All of a sudden, the box underneath me gave way, and I lost my balance. I put out my arm to break my fall. A long, spiked pole from a display unit that was mounted on the floor went into the upper part of my arm, and pushed its way inward toward my shoulder. According to the x-rays that I would later receive, the spike just missed my lung. Standing up, somewhat dazed, I pulled it out. Although there was a limited amount of bleeding, it was incredibly painful and obvious that the wound was deep. I immediately went to the front of the store to find the foreman. I asked if someone would drive me to the hospital. The foreman was quite unsympathetic to my plight and since no one was able to leave the shift, it was apparent that I would have to drive myself to emergency. There, they x-rayed my arm, probed it, and felt that nothing had broken off inside; they were satisfied enough to send me home. My arm was put in a sling. By then my shoulder had swelled up, and it was difficult for me even to sit in a comfortable position.

I left emergency and drove home, arriving several hours earlier than normal. I immediately went to bed in pain and exhaustion. The next morning my mother came into my room somewhat concerned that I had arrived home early. She was startled to see the injury. My shoulder was swollen, and part of my neck was black and blue. My father appeared in the room and was obviously quite concerned. However, he was not able to express his emotions and went to work as usual that morning. Several hours later, my mother also went to work in the family business.

For the entire day, I stayed home. At one point I did not hear the telephone ring, as I was sleeping. The call was from my father, trying to contact me to see how I was doing. Since I did not answer his call, he became extremely worried. He walked the short distance from work as quickly as he could. He arrived home out of breath, and seeing me, came over and embraced me. He stated that he was very concerned, and since no one had answered the phone, he wondered if something had happened to me. Being the typical teenager that I was, I pulled back from his embrace. I felt uncomfortable.

After my father spoke with me for a few minutes and felt reassured, he returned to work.

Even now I feel sad that I did not seize the opportunity to appreciate my father's concern and to thank him. As a teenager it was natural for me to push him away. It is now easier to understand his sense of caring and the way he expressed it. At that time, it was not.

When my older sister died several years earlier, she was the same age as I was at the time of this accident. My father had never come to terms with her death, and I believe he was quite anxious about me and my health at that age. To my father, his son was now moving into a new era — I was to turn eighteen soon, an age that my sister did not reach. My father was not sure what the next step was. I can understand now how anxious he must have felt.

At one time, we felt that it was not manly to express feelings or to demonstrate nurturing feelings. There was an unconscious discouragement of sorts. Now we can say it: fathers have feelings too, and it is okay to show them to others, especially your child. A child wants to be touched and held.

For me, the ultimate masculine experience is to become a father. And an integral part of being a father is the ability to express how you feel, especially with your child.

RUNNING THE GOOD RACE

As I rounded the corner of the track, I looked up. I saw him rise from his seat in the stands and wave his arms. He blocked out the sun like a giant. He was cheering loudly as I ran toward the finish line. This was my graduation year, the last time I would run for my high school track team. I was unfamiliar with steeplechase races, yet I had outrun the entire field. As I burst through the finish line, my father came out onto the track and hugged me, proud of what I had achieved. However, *I* didn't win that race. We won it together.

The race was momentous for me in several ways. Not only was it the last race I would run for my high school, but

I was also turning eighteen, coming of age. I was entering adulthood. My father had always stood behind me in all of my endeavours. Over the years, as I was running long-distance races, he was my number one fan.

That race was the culmination of me and my father working together. A month prior to the event, my high school coach had requested that I enter the newly introduced steeplechase race rather than the two-mile race I had been training for. I had no idea what running a steeplechase race entailed. The coach gave me a training manual that was a number of years out of date and not very helpful. I mentioned all of this to my father, who at the outset said very little. However, unbeknownst to me, he travelled to the next city, located the stadium there, found a steeplechase jump, measured it, came home, and built four of them for me. In order to do this, he tore down a trellis that he had constructed several years earlier at the side of the house. The jumps were measured exactly to size and painted exactly like the ones he had seen in the stadium. This enabled me to train for several weeks with the right type of apparatus and to understand the techniques I needed to perfect.

This was the unspoken partnership between my father and me: his willingness to quietly support my aspirations and to find a concrete way to help me achieve them. This is what I mean when I say that he was as much the winner of that race as I was.

My father and I grew into our roles together, a journey we shared throughout my childhood and adolescence. Men don't become fathers by some magical process of just knowing what to do or by just being there. They become fathers by being involved. I, as the son, taught the man how to father, and he taught me how to grow up and become a man.

A man starts the fathering journey in earnest as he enters adulthood. From the time of his partner's first pregnancy, he has the opportunity to construct for himself a model of involved fathering. When he reaches the stage of eventually becoming a grandfather, he is the elder who provides leadership to the following generations. "Father" is not a noun, it is a verb. "Father" is not something you are, it is something you do. In building those steeplechase jumps for me, he was *doing* — he was fathering.

Despite the long hours he worked and his uncertainty as to exactly how he should involve himself in the lives of his children, it slowly dawned on him as he grew into his fathering role that if he could join his children in their play, then he would become a good father. My mother encouraged him in this and supported him in the process.

This playfulness took many different forms during the years I was growing up, and it provided him with an alternative to simply being a hard worker. Through play, he learned to engage himself in his children's lives. Everyone saw him as a friendly man who was fun to be with. On occasion, my father would tell my mother that he did not really know how to interact with his children. But when he didn't think about it, and just let himself be there, that's all that really mattered. As he grew with me over the years, he became more intuitive in identifying what it was that I needed. By the time of my last year of high school, as I was entering adulthood, he joined me in that transition to manhood. When I crossed the finish line, it was he and I together. I had only made it that far because he had known, as a father, how to meet my needs.

So many men say they don't know what to do as fathers. But if they allow themselves to relax and play, and ask themselves, "If I were my son or daughter, what would I want my father to do with me or for me?" they will be surprised at all the possibilities that emerge. Most often, what the child wants, more than anything, is just for dad to be interested in him or her, to be involved with him or her at that moment. Understanding fathering as a process rather than as a fixed state of being makes a difference both to the man and to the child.

FROM CHILD TO ADULT

My father was a modest man who never bragged about what he had. In fact, he said very little about himself at all. He was very self-conscious, especially of his body. He never felt comfortable wearing shorts, for instance, because he was so thin and he had varicose veins. He always seemed to be covering himself.

When my father and I went to public swimming pools, he would enter into another room beside the locker room and change there quickly. Then he would head directly for the pool and immediately jump in.

His hiding was also noticeable in social situations. When we attended family gatherings, he would stay in the background. When he was with groups of other people in public, he seldom expressed his own opinions.

At first I accepted this behaviour as normal. Likewise, I naturally imitated him.

As I entered puberty, I felt myself increasingly uncomfortable with the changes occurring to my body. In grade seven I wanted to hide in order to avoid taking a shower with the other boys after gym class. I was afraid that someone might see me.

It was also about this time that I became curious about where babies actually came from. There were many different explanations, but they did not make sense to me. One spring evening when my father and I were doing some work on a retaining wall at home, I asked him this very question. He hesitated, then answered quite brusquely, "From the hospital."

Several weeks later, my father and I were in the car. We were on our way to a sex education evening for boys at the local high school. I guess he figured out it was time. As we were driving along, I asked him more questions about babies and inquired if what happens to girls on a monthly basis also happens to boys. I had no clear idea of sexuality or what sex meant. My father was very uncomfortable, and again his answers did not address the questions. The film that my father and I saw at the school confused me even more. Eventually, over the next several months, I discovered from my friends and from books what I wanted to know regarding entering manhood, body changes, wet dreams, masturbation, and sex . . . and where babies come from.

I don't hold my father's reticence against him. He was doing his best and had his own self-image problems to contend with. And, in the end, the way he treated my questions helped me decide how to handle the sex question with my own children.

Prior to the birth of our daughters, my wife and I discussed the importance of helping our children to understand themselves and their bodies, and to understand femininity and masculinity. We also decided that when the time was appropriate we would talk with them about sex. We felt it important to be as open as reasonably possible to any questions they might have.

This feeling continues as we promote an atmosphere of openness and frankness in which our daughters can approach us to discuss these important issues. We have encouraged questions and have answered with age-appropriate responses, sometimes together, sometimes one-on-one.

My father helped me see that I must forge a strong identity for myself, which could then become the foundation for talking about sex to my daughters. Settling this issue early is important, as children today are subjected to a barrage of sex from TV, especially in music videos and advertisements.

How comfortable are you with yourself? With your identity? Do you understand who you are? Your sexuality? How do you express your masculinity? Are you in charge of your history, or is your history in charge of you? Remember, your child is watching you, learning from you, and understanding him/herself through you.

LET'S NOT TALK

My teenage years coincided with the acting out of youth in the rebellious 1960s. I grew my hair long and was quite active in a variety of protest movements. My bedroom wall was plastered with posters of rock groups and radical political causes. My room itself was often in disarray. I became more and more distant from my father throughout those years. In fact, there was a time when I looked at him in a negative, condescending way.

Once, during a federal election campaign, I expressed some of my typical adolescent frustration and anger toward authority. Leaning politically to the left at that time, I contacted the campaign headquarters of the Marxist–Leninist candidate in our riding and asked that his sign be placed on our front lawn. My request was gratefully accepted and eagerly acted on. The sign they erected was very large and very noticeable.

When my father arrived home from work that evening and entered the driveway, the sign immediately caught his eye. He was furious. Although his political adherence was similar to mine (though not to the same extreme), this sign was a little too much for him. He wasted no time in telling me that I had one week to take the sign off the lawn.

As much as my father discouraged this over-enthusiastic sort of expression, he did support my need to act out and to demonstrate my independence in other ways. The style of any teenager was to wear army jackets and jeans with rips, tears, and patches. I recall taking the train to Toronto with my father, walking into an army surplus store, and purchasing such a jacket. He knew it was important for me to feel that I fit in.

During this same trip, he took me to a pawnshop and bought me an expensive wristwatch. Even though our family did not have a great deal of money, my father instinctively knew that this was important for me. I no longer have the jacket, but I have kept the watch.

My father and I struggled to communicate during those years. We were often at odds on any number of issues. I found it difficult to speak to him about personal matters. There were times when I felt I needed to have secrets. On occasion I would come close to scorning him. I would challenge him on what I called his "middle-class sitting-on-the-fence values" and made remarks about his appearance.

Through it all, he never raised his voice or argued. He appeared to be willing to discuss my point of view if I wanted to talk with him about it.

Despite his anger over the sign, he gave me a week to take it down. He needed to set a limit regarding my behaviour, but he also realized the need for me to have a period of time in which to act out. I believe he understood this need even during the times that communication between us had broken down. He seemed to feel it was best just to be there and be available to me in case I wanted to talk.

I now experience the same situation with my fifteen year old daughter. There are times when she becomes defiant or angry and walks out of the room. It is understandable; I know that she needs to do it. The worst thing I could do is follow her and immediately discuss the issue at hand. If I give things some time, and a little distance, we are usually able to sit down and talk it out. There are certain matters, however, that *need* to become secrets. She *should* be uncomfortable talking to me about them.

The close personal relationship that you have established with your child over the years comes strongly into play during the teen years. Your child knows, deep down, that there is still some degree of connectedness — even during times when you are not talking.

You may not talk as much, but you can still communicate. When you make it clear that you are available, that you are listening, that you will be available when you are approached, you are communicating. When you are approached, you join your child while still allowing his or her own sense of individuality.

Adolescents need to identify with others and make them a part of themselves to help foster their independence. These times may create the feeling that your child is being distant from you or of having been shut out of his or her life. You can count on this: by being friendly, responsive, and available for conversation, your child knows there is a relationship to come back to.

TIME ALONE TOGETHER

My father and I travelled by train to the 1976 Olympics in Montreal to watch some of the events. I was in my early twenties and in graduate school. My father was in his late sixties. We spent several days at the Olympics and touring Montreal, travelling back and forth on subway trains. There had not been many times that we had been alone together, enjoying a common interest like this. This was one of the last times that we would do so. Shortly after the trip, I would move away from home to pursue my career.

At different times during the trip we spoke about my father's family, how he felt about retirement, the direction

I was taking in my university studies, my job searches and, of course, the Olympics, among other things. However, it was not just the conversation that was important, it was spending time with my father, just the two of us.

Throughout both of my daughters' first years, I found it rewarding to take them with me when I would go on errands, or occasionally take them with me when I went to work. There were also numerous times when I would just take them for a walk in a stroller — around the block or to the park. I was fortunate that my employment situation provided me with the opportunity to take either of my daughters to my office for part of the day.

There were also times when I would stay with them alone at home, sometimes because my wife was at work or attending a conference out of town, sometimes because I just chose to be there with them. I discovered that I could throw a sponge in the sink or turn the light switch off and on to entertain them, and that an hour or two would quickly pass by. Both of my daughters enjoyed these simple activities at that age, and I found it an easy way to engage with them.

As they grew, I realized that it was actually quite easy to invent numerous fun games for my daughters, whether at home, in the car, or elsewhere. It did not take long for them to involve themselves in these games with me. As they grew, they often looked to my creativity, or they expressed their own, as we developed new ways of playing together. When Ailène was two years of age and in-line skating had become the new fad, I would often put her pink tricycle helmet on her head, buckle her into the baby carriage, strap on my in-line skates, and take off, pushing the carriage. She thoroughly enjoyed these excursions and would point her finger in the direction she wanted to go. I found that if I could adapt myself to my daughters' interests, we readily enjoyed one another's company.

As my two daughters grew and became more creative and ambitious in their play, it became necessary for me to engage with them in more elaborate activities that took more planning. One extremely snowy winter, for example, I built a sled run on an incline beside our home. Ailène was nine and Alexandra was three. Late at night, I sprayed water on the run so it would make it icier for them and increase their speed when they used it the next day. I obtained a number of bales of straw from a friend and placed them along the edge of the run for safety. I also built up the banks with a great deal of snow. Both of my daughters put on their bicycle helmets, and the older one lay down on the sled on her stomach. The younger one would then climb on top of her sister's back and hold onto her shoulders. They would ask me to give them a push, and off they went.

We had a great deal of fun doing this despite the amount of work involved for me. I am not a handyman or an engineer by nature, so I learned how to build the sled run on the job. My daughters gave me ideas and participated in its construction. I enjoyed going down the run with them, and the winter passed by quickly. My wife, our two daughters, and I would often spend a weekend afternoon sledding. It did not take long for the word to get out to other children in the neighbourhood that they were invited to go down this sled run as well. Numerous friends of my daughters came over and played for hours.

Another way I found time alone with my daughters was to take them on a vacation for several days, sometimes even up to a week. It started when Ailène was eight. This time alone has come to mean a great deal to all three of us.

Finding ways of spending time alone with my children as they have grown has been both challenging and rewarding. I quickly discovered that all I really had to do was observe what they enjoyed doing or wanted to do and then figure out ways we could participate in those activities together.

I have many fond memories of playing catch with my father. He and I also went golfing and worked together around the home or in the family business. These times together were very special for me, as I got to be alone with my father. For a son or daughter to have these moments alone with dad means a great deal. Both a father and a child need opportunities to be alone and to experience each other.

For the father, it assists in his role as a parent and contributes to a better understanding of himself and how he fathers the next generation. It also provides him with increased feelings of confidence and competence in what he is doing.

For the child, this time alone provides him or her with a very important model apart from the mother. It gives them the opportunity to experience nurturing from a masculine perspective.

My father's participation in my life, whether it was driving me to school, building me a steeplechase jump, travelling to the Olympics, or going on family vacations, was a way for him to join me in my interests. There were other numerous ways that he and I were able to involve ourselves in each other's lives. My father appeared to be happy just observing my participation in various activities as well. He did not necessarily have to join in all of them, all the time. I believe my father learned for himself a way that he could engage in my life and at the same time understand what it was that I needed to meet both my own needs and those of interacting with others.

As a society, we now have more leisure time than my father's generation did. This time provides us with the opportunity to engage with our children in numerous activities. By being actively involved with the child, we are able to become a part of them and join with them and what they are involved in. The more time we are able to spend with them, the better we can understand what it is they need and help to provide that for them.

It can start with throwing a sponge in the sink or turning a light switch off and on, and then watch how fast the time goes by! If a person engages in the play activity and does not worry about outside pressures or work responsibilities, moments pass most pleasurably.

It is special for father and child to be alone together. This time provides a father with the opportunity to see these developmental moments in the child's life. Fond memories are created. These alone-times together give your child a special feeling that they will carry throughout a lifetime.

GOD?

My father was born into a very devout Presbyterian family tradition. The rural church his family attended joined with a Methodist congregation when he was quite young. Later it became a United Church. My father was reared in a strict belief system based on the Protestant work ethic. His parents were active in numerous church-related activities, including singing in the choir, attending Bible study, and teaching Sunday school. For my father and his family, the church was the focal point of their social lives. It provided him with strong moral values — values to which he would adhere throughout his life.

During the Depression in the 1930s, my father was forced to leave this tight-knit, rural community, as well as the farm on which he was raised, to seek employment in urban areas. While working as a relief operator at a railway station in Kitchener, Ontario, he met my mother. Her religious background was Lutheran and more liberal than his. My father was able to adapt to a more flexible religious lifestyle when he married my mother and became involved in a Lutheran church.

My spiritual upbringing was a coming-together of these two religious backgrounds. In my family, there was a strong attachment to religious beliefs. This was tempered, however, with tolerance toward others' beliefs. As a young man I attended a Lutheran seminary and graduated with a Master of Divinity degree. During my seminary years, I dated a Jewish woman. My father, to his credit, was tolerant of this inter-religious relationship, which in any case did not last.

After seminary and prior to my marriage, I found myself less inclined to follow institutionalized religion. I decided to pursue studies in social work instead of becoming a minister. As my wife had no specific religious adherence, we felt comfortable exposing our daughters to a variety of religions.

Upon reflection of my religious past and present, I feel that I may have moved too far from a structured religious perspective. As I speak to my daughters about religious matters, or as they ask me questions about religion, I am aware of the need to provide both of them with a framework in which they will be able to develop their own religious beliefs. This religious framework is what I view as defining one's sense of one's own integrity. Integrity, as I see it, is made up of a firm attachment to morality, honesty, and sincerity.

Let's view religion and integrity from another perspective. If you exercised your right leg only, your right leg would become overdeveloped, and your left leg underdeveloped. Obviously, it would be difficult to walk at all. If a dad is too rigid and moralistic, or perhaps too flexible and permissive, an imbalance will occur. The question is whether our beliefs or faith are balanced.

FAMILY FIRST

My father lay motionless in his bed, in a fetal position, as if asleep. I held his hand and touched his face. He died the way he wanted to: in his bed, at home, surrounded by family. He was in his ninetieth year.

My father was born in a family farmhouse on the kitchen table. The next-door neighbour came from several miles away by horse and buggy to be the midwife. My grandfather and uncle waited on the veranda outside, doing what they could to help out.

My father's family moved only once, and that was when he was a young boy. They moved several farms over. Everybody in the community knew each other, and they often met weekly, either in the town market or at church. The families were very supportive of each other and worked quite hard, especially through the difficult period of the Depression.

Living and working on the farm meant that what you planted, you then harvested and, for the most part, consumed. The family worked together in the fields and saw the fruits of their labours. At that time, few in my father's community actually worked away from the farm. However, with the Depression, it was necessary for my father to seek employment elsewhere. He worked for the railway as a telegrapher, coming home on the weekends. This added income helped to support his family.

My father met my mother at one of the stations where he was working. They eventually married and moved into the city. They had three children: my two sisters and me.

City life was quite different for my father. He had to adapt quickly. He brought with him the value of hard work and, like his family of origin, he chose to move only once with our family. When I was a small boy we moved down the street. My father actually turned down promotions with the railway so that he could remain local, commuting back and forth to his place of employment so that his family did not have to move.

I remember many events that we engaged in as a family. Yearly, we would go to the beach. On a number of occasions, we took family vacations travelling across Canada. When my younger sister or I worked in other parts of the country, my parents would often come to visit. My father in particular made a point of trying to understand situations that my sister and I were experiencing and living in, and helped us out in any way he could.

With the opportunities available to my sister and I, and increased leisure activity in general in society, we have experienced more flexibility and distractions to do other things than my father did. However, my father felt it important to keep his roots and remain constant. As he entered retirement, he and my mother moved into a condominium unit. It was built on the same spot where they had lived in an apartment years before when they were first married. It was as if he had come full circle.

It was in that condo that my father died, among his family.

A rich value that my father taught me was the importance of putting family first; of remaining family-centred. Yes, it was necessary for him to sacrifice. However, this was not a struggle for him. He identified himself as a father first and accepted whatever came with that. It was all part of the package, and those responsibilities were to be followed through on.

Doing things as a family means that a father needs to be flexible and adapt to the different demands and challenges that he faces. A father is always under construction. He is aware of how the children are growing into different life stages and of his need to lead or participate in different activities or events to enhance this growth. Security and stability, and their father being there, is important for children as they grow.

Today's family is continually dealing with a noisy background and is constantly affected by social change. Our family systems are more fluid than ever before. We have more of a variety of things we can do than what was experienced by my father's generation. However, one value remains, and that is the importance of family and its need to come first.

BURIED IN MY HEART

I had finished a presentation on fathering at a parenting conference for public health nurses and their colleagues several years ago. After answering a number of questions I excused myself, as I had to leave the conference early to catch my flight home.

As I walked toward the main entrance, I heard someone call out my name. I turned around and saw a friend that I had known in my university days standing there. She was now a public health nurse and had been attending the conference. We hugged each other and spoke briefly about what each of us was doing. Unfortunately, I was in a hurry and the conversation was rushed. As we spoke about what we had been doing over the years and our family situations, it felt like old times for me. I still felt a great deal of fondness for her.

As I was about to say goodbye, she suddenly inquired about my father and how he was doing. She had become quite attached to him during those few years that we were together in university. As her father had died when she was quite young, she had readily engaged with my father. She found him an easy-going, laid-back individual and related to him easily. My father had accepted her as family and enjoyed talking to her. I told her sadly that he had died only several months prior, at the age of eighty-nine. She took the news hard and chokingly expressed her sympathy. For a few seconds there was silence between us. Then she asked where my father was buried, which I told her. She said that she would be travelling through that area in the next several months and would like to visit the gravesite.

We looked at each other without saying a word. Again we hugged, then parted in silence. There was so much left to be said, and yet, what more could we say to each other? As I walked toward the exit, I realized that I had not told her the truth about where my father was buried. My father wasn't buried in that cemetery; my father is buried in my heart.

As we grow through the teen years, it is important for us to identify with a person, or persons. We take aspects of their characteristics or personalities into ourselves and imitate them to some degree. However, this identification doesn't just begin at adolescence; it intensifies during that time, but it is an ongoing process throughout life.

It starts between the baby and the parents. The baby begins to identify with and take aspects of each parent into his or her personality. By taking in aspects of another person, we carry a part of them inside us. This is a normal developmental process in life that guides us along the pathway of interactions with others. These identifications influence the decisions we make, the way we are, and how able we are to empathize with others. Through the years, we internalize numerous aspects of many different people from many different walks of life, including and beyond our families. Some individuals obviously have a greater impact on us than others, especially those closer to us.

Part of being an involved, responsible father is being able to share and lend part of yourself to others, most importantly to your children. A child takes a part of you inside of him or her as they develop and establish their own sense of identity, their own selfhood. However, you need to be there to be taken in, to be internalized. The types of behaviour you exhibit and the way you interact with your child all leave an imprint upon them.

As a son, I identified with my father. I watched his behaviour — the ways he interacted with others and with me, as well as his ability to empathize, to listen to others, and to feel with them. I also observed his interactions with my mother and sisters, as well as other females that he met in his life. It was through these observations that I learned how to treat women with respect. My father became a part of me through this identification process. Whether he handled situations maturely or immaturely, all left an imprint on my psyche.

Now, how I interact with my wife, how I father my children, and how I involve myself with others around me has been greatly influenced by how he fathered me. Perhaps the most magical moments are the times when I feel as if I am my father in my interactions with my children.

BECOMING DAD

They appeared so helpless lying there. Each one was tiny, crying, purplish in colour, arms and legs flailing about. Until this moment every one of their needs had been met on demand and each was in a safe and secure environment. Now everything was so different. Bright lights, noise, temperature change, and even air! Both of my daughters' births — six years apart from each other — were nothing less than miraculous, and watching each of them being born left me on an adrenaline high. I felt excited and proud, and I could not help but wonder if their features would be like mine. I also felt a tremendous responsibility — they each needed me now and *forever*. This was my first true Dad moment.

Each of my daughters was placed gently in their mother's arms, swaddled in delivery blankets with little pink caps on their heads. I first touched the backs of their hands and then their faces. It had been a long nine months for all of us. Throughout the first trimester of both pregnancies, my wife was very ill and unable to go to work. Her diet seemed to be made up primarily of Popsicles and fluids. In the second trimester, as I attended ultrasound visits and prenatal check-ups, I was able to see the shadow of what appeared to be my daughter "in there." The ultrasound image almost seemed alien. All of these events and more brought me closer to the pregnancy picture and contributed each time to my sense of becoming a father. By the third trimester the nursery had been set up, and my wife needed me to assist her more often with sometimes very routine tasks. During this time in the first pregnancy, I attended prenatal classes and quickly realized the importance of listening to other men's stories as they became fathers. When I heard them speak, I no longer felt that I was alone.

Soon the moment approached that we had all been looking forward to, and in that moment I was suddenly Dad.

Throughout the nine months leading up to the birth, and especially as anticipation sets in during the final trimester, the soon-to-be father is almost overwhelmed by the variety of feelings he experiences. There is so much going on, and attention to the mother's health is primary. This range of feelings includes concern, anxiety, ambivalence, confusion, excitement, relief, and joy. All of these feelings are natural and normal, and are part of the developmental process that leads toward the transition into parenthood.

The most dramatic Dad moment occurs at that point of birth, when you see your baby for the very first time. You become engrossed with him or her. You suddenly realize, for a very brief moment, that your total focus is on your baby. You feel as if you have neglected your partner, the person whose well-being you had been very concerned about for the past several hours. Do not be alarmed. What is happening to you is that there are suddenly two people in your life that you have responsibility toward. Baby and mother. You are now a family; there is now another person in your life who needs you and who is very much a part of you. You are a father who will be needed throughout all of your child's life. This relationship is *for life*.

FATHER TO BE

While attending prenatal classes with my wife prior to the birth of our first daughter, I realized how little I knew about my upcoming role of father. As I started these classes, I felt that the content was focused more on moms. We men were there to learn how to be supportive of them. The nurse/instructor told me in the class that I was a coach. I took that to mean that I could pretty well leave everything up to my wife. She would interpret to me what I needed to do or to understand. I subscribed to the idea that parenting is mothering and that I was to follow my wife's lead, whether it was through this prenatal time, birthing, or after the birth. She would tell me how to be a parent.

So for the first several classes, I did what I was told. I helped my wife practice her breathing techniques and relaxation exercises. However, things would quickly change for me as the classes progressed. In the fifth class, we were informed that in the following week's class we would be going to the local hospital. We would tour the birthing and mother–baby units. A father who was sitting at the back of the class — a rather large, quiet man — asked if there would be any blood in the delivery room while we were on the tour. The class chuckled. The instructor assured him that there would be no blood. However, you could see that her reassurance did not fully convince him.

Shortly thereafter, we took a break. The mothers gathered together at the front of the classroom and spoke about how they were feeling, expressing anxiety regarding the births. The fathers went out into the hallway and scattered around the pop machine. While we talked, someone would occasionally kick the side of the machine, as if kicking the tire of a car. I spoke to the father who had expressed concern about blood in the delivery room and, ever the therapist, asked him what was really bothering him. He informed me that even though he faints at the sight of blood, passing out was not what he was concerned about. He was worried that he would miss the birth of his child. This comment immediately tempered the humour we had felt when he had expressed his concern. His statement pointed out to me that expectant fathers have their own feelings and anxieties, and that such concerns are just as much a part of the prenatal and birthing equation as those of mothers. However, it is easy to overlook this, and in this class, our concerns were not addressed.

From this class experience I developed a program called "Dad Classes." Each class series centres on issues and concerns that an expectant father (or new father) has in his relationship with his partner, with his baby, and with himself. The series has been very successful during the past ten years and over a thousand fathers have attended and completed the classes. In the last week of each series, the moms are invited to attend. On several occasions babies who have been born during the class series have also been present. A nurse from the hospital's mother–baby unit also attends this week. Work is done with the mothers and fathers, both separately and together as couples.

The Dad Class series examines how a man builds an involved fathering model for himself. He is encouraged to discover his own style in relating to his baby, including the picking up and holding of the baby. This style is different than the mother's way. No *Mr. Mom* or babysitter images exist in these classes.

The important prenatal period can be likened to a journey in a canoe across a lake. The couple, mother and father, climb in together and begin paddling. They share a goal, which is to reach a specific landing spot. While paddling across the lake, the mother goes through different trimester periods. As the journey progresses, and both mother and father develop and change, the canoe loses equilibrium. It becomes necessary for the couple to stop paddling and to examine their positions in the canoe. The transition to parenthood has begun for them. They may need to stop the canoe completely, safely shift their positions, or do something altogether different.

By comparison, in the prenatal period during the first trimester, the father is drawn slowly further into the situation by being aware of how the mother is feeling. By the second trimester, as she begins to show, the father, who may have attended prenatal visits and ultrasounds, is now able to see "in there." Many fathers find the ultrasound experience exciting, as they can actually see their babies. In the third trimester, a mother relies more on the father to be there to help her out with specific tasks or chores. The mother is finding it increasingly difficult to get herself comfortable and to be able to do certain things. She needs to feel the security that comes with her partner being close by. This third trimester, a time of anticipation, brings the father into the final pre-birth process.

Throughout this prenatal period, or the journey in the canoe so to speak, the father has a wonderful opportunity to engage in the transition to parenthood and to prepare both himself and his partner for the changes that are about to take place in their lives. They are able to work together in securing the appropriate landing spot for the canoe. However, only a father who is there and who is involved is able to achieve this.

Fathers have their own styles, their own ways of involving themselves with their babies. A father who actively participates in the prenatal and birthing process has the opportunity to develop this style. His participation helps to facilitate his feelings of confidence and self-worth. It makes him feel more competent as he makes the transition from manhood into fatherhood.

There are many ways that an expectant father is able to achieve these feelings. For example, he can attend prenatal checkups, ultrasound visits, breast feeding classes, prenatal classes, and Dad Classes. There are more opportunities now for a man to be involved in the prenatal period, both by himself and with his partner, than ever before.

As the canoe reaches the landing point on the other side of the lake and the journey draws to a conclusion, a new journey begins. That journey is parenthood.

The more a man involves himself with the journey into fatherhood, the more he feels able to involve himself as a father.

MY FATHER, MY DAUGHTERS, AND ME

S hortly after my father's death, I found a box of photographs that were tucked away in the back of his closet. As I went through them, I found one picture of my father holding me in his arms when I was approximately five months of age. It was an old black and white photograph that appeared to have been taken outside of the family home on a winter's day. My father was wearing his suit and holding me in a rigid manner, tilting and posing me toward my mother, who held the camera. It appeared as if he had just returned from work and would need to go back shortly. I looked as if I had just been pulled off the breast and was in a drowsy state, with my eyes half open and my mouth searching for something to suck on. I was quite bundled up. My father did not appear to be comfortable holding me, and it was as if I had been propped up in his arms for this picture.

When my older daughter was five months of age, my father volunteered to feed her the usual bottle of soy milk. After she was finished the bottle, my father carefully laid her over his shoulder and walked gingerly about the room. Instead of patting Ailène on the back to induce a burp, he felt it best that she was not to move at all. This reflected his uncertainty in holding her. My father was concerned that if he was to move her, she might throw up, so he especially did not want to pat her back.

However, his nightmare came true. My daughter, with great gusto, threw up the entire contents of the bottle all over my father's back, the living room couch, and the floor. My father was stunned. This messy situation was only compounding his discomfort in holding Ailène.

However, this experience did not deter him from helping out with feeding my second daughter, Alexandra. He had gained confidence in holding babies by then, and was very dutiful in burping her from time to time as she fed. He was very proud of the fact that she did not throw up after the feeding. She went to sleep in his arms quite contentedly.

When I was born (in the 1950s), fathers had limited experiences in touching or holding their children, especially when they were babies. For that reason, my father was uncertain and felt awkward about holding me. He left most of this up to my mother. Over the years, though, things have changed. As I became a father, I realized the importance of getting used to holding my daughters. I noticed that the more I did this, the more confident I felt about myself, and it soon became quite natural for me.

My father, even though he had become a grandfather, still carried with him that old script of feeling uncertain and awkward when he held a baby. As he got more used to it and he witnessed other men, especially his son, holding a baby though, it became second nature to him. He found it easier to pick Ailène up and hold her, and he frequently volunteered to do so.

My father's initial approach to involving himself with a baby — whether it was me, or later when he was a grandfather — was a goal-oriented one. It was either to hold me up to the camera or to get the formula into my daughter. These were the tasks that needed to be achieved. He was not able to relax and enjoy the experiences of holding and feeding. For my father, it was a job had to be done, and that was all.

In the past, the father felt that he had an expected role to perform. Part of that role meant limited involvement. Fortunately, these attitudes have been changing in our society over the past several decades, and today's fathers are able to be much more flexible.

The more you can be involved with your baby, the more competent and confident you feel as a father. It is okay to enjoy feeding times with your baby. It is not changing the diaper that matters, but your attitudes and feelings toward the changing. This is the state of the new fatherhood.

As men, we have been encouraged — and almost expected — to be stiff, to conform to rules, and to express no spontaneity. Societal expectations have been restrictive. As we enter fatherhood, it is easy to carry some of these values and expectations with us. Yet, within us we have the ability to be caring, nurturing persons to our children. It is difficult to lighten up, but we need to do so in order to enjoy just being with our children.

As a father, you have — or will have — your own way of involving yourself with your child. Explore that way, become comfortable with it, and allow it to be a natural part of your special relationship with your child.

FATHER AND MOTHER

My parents would sometimes hold hands in public or kiss each other in front of me, but these romantic actions were guarded, almost secretive. I had not thought about this until a romantic moment between my wife and I got our girls giggling.

It was a lovely fall day and as a family we were enjoying the time together walking through a large theme park. As it was the middle of the week, there was little crowd to contend with. Access to most shows and rides was very easy. Our daughters were much younger then, and we were having a wonderful time on our walk. Each turn in the path created new excitement as to what activity, ride, or cartoon character they might encounter. As they ran on ahead of us, my wife and I walked along holding hands. Suddenly Ailène turned around, looked at us, and tried to mask her smile. She quickly ran over to Alexandra and whispered something to her. Alexandra, likewise, looked at us and started to laugh. I asked them what it was that they found so amusing. They both said in teasing voices, "Daddy and Mommy are holding hands."

At that moment I recalled my own parents holding hands and my reaction, as well as another time where both my daughters saw me kiss my wife prior to going to work. Again at that time they both giggled and I could hear another teasing comment.

What are your attitudes and feelings toward women? Do you support and respect the mother of your child? How do you exhibit emotions, express your feelings, and demonstrate your sensitivity toward her and with her?

My daughters are quite aware of the relationship between their mother and their father. How we interact with each other is observed by them, and they quickly pick up on even the smallest nuances. How a dad reacts to and treats a mom and vice versa imprints upon them how a man and a woman should relate. How a dad shows respect for other women and the way he treats them also leaves an imprint.

All of these observed experiences contribute to the type of partner they will become involved with in later life and how they will treat or be treated by other people. Remember, you are being watched.

THE FIRST TIME

I accompanied my daughter Ailène to preschool on her first day. It was a half-day, five-days-a-week program at the local Jewish Community Centre. She was three and a half years old at the time. As we entered the classroom, she quickly glanced around and immediately started to play with several of the other children. I told her I would be leaving and would be back at noon to pick her up. We gave each other a hug. She was very excited. Sitting at a small table, she hastily waved goodbye to me with a large wooden spoon. She was ready to play.

As I left the building where the school was located, I turned around. There against the outside wall were several mothers and another father huddled together. It was evident that we were all having trouble separating from our children that first morning.

When I went to pick her up at noon, she told me that she had had a lot of fun and asked if she would be going back there again tomorrow. I said yes. She then asked if I would stay with her. I said that it would be fun to play with her but I wouldn't be able to stay. I would pick her up at noon as I did today.

That night at home Ailène was quite upset. It was difficult for her to understand that I would be taking her back to the school and leaving her there by herself with the other children.

The next morning it took her awhile to get going. On the drive to school, she was extremely quiet. Once we arrived at the school, she started to cry. She hung onto my hand, insisting that I stay. I told her that I would be back at noon again to pick her up. One of the teachers, sensing the difficulty we were both having, immediately came over. She gave my daughter a rather snug bear hug and pointed me toward the door. I made my exit. Within a day, Ailène had settled in to being at school and the rest is history.

Almost the same scenario happened with my other daughter, Alexandra, when she started going to school for the first time.

It was difficult for me to say goodbye, as I had been such a part of the daily activities of both of my daughters. Now there was actually some time when they were in their own place involved with something interesting to them. I was somewhere else. Like Ailène, Alexandra also had fun that first morning and then, realizing that I would not be staying with her the next day, became quite upset. However, Alexandra soon settled into the routine and had fun attending school like her sister had before her.

There are many other firsts that I recall in both my daughters' lives. I am glad I was able to participate in or be there for them. One such incident was the first time I took Ailène to a birthday party and her outfit included her mother's shoes. I remember how it felt saying goodbye to her as she went in to play with the other children. I once stayed with Alexandra at a birthday party she was invited to and watched her as she lined up at the buffet with the other children, plate in hand, selecting food for herself. This had been something that either her mother or I would have done for her in the past. Now she was doing it on her own.

There were so many other firsts, far too many to list, and I know that there were some that I missed. It would be impossible to attend them all. However, whether it was observing the first tooth, hearing the first word, helping with the first walk, swimming, riding a bike, shooting a basketball into the net, reading, or many, many other events, both Alexandra and Ailène were excited and proud to achieve these milestones and even prouder to share them with Mom and Dad.

I found that when both of my daughters were younger and growing quickly through many stages, they wanted me frequently involved in their lives. As they grew older, there were times when they did not want me there as much. They wanted to experience feelings of self-mastery and of being on their own. However, in order to achieve such feelings, it was important for them to feel that I had been there in the first place. In a sense, I had helped provide them with a secure base that they could stand on. They each learned to internalize parts of our relationship, as well as a part of me. This would enable them to do more things for themselves. So in a strange way, even though I am not with them at certain times, there is a part of me that is inside each of them when they are on their own, and a part of each of them inside of me.

It is not reasonable to expect a father to be there all the time with his child. There are many firsts a father will miss. I found, however, that the more firsts I could experience, the better able I was to participate in my children's development. This helped me to understand how they were growing and changing each day.

On numerous occasions when I was at work, I found myself thinking about my daughters and what they were doing. One time I suddenly realized that they were spending their lives in one place (such as school) and I was somewhere else (work). It is as necessary to be apart at times as it is to be together. However, I realize that I took those days for granted, especially when they started attending school full time. It has become easy to see that the days passed into weeks, and then into months, and suddenly the school year was over.

It was at that point that I made a conscious effort to at least consider spending one day every several months with my children in their classrooms at school, joining in with their activities. As Ailène reached a higher grade, I would assist the teacher in any way I could. Occasionally when I had time, I would volunteer to drive their classmates to various activities. To be able to do this, I would need to schedule the day I would be at the school well in advance and make sure I wrote it down in my planner. I felt that this was a way that I could remain balanced between family and work and look forward to those days when I could connect with my children in their own environment. However, it was not always possible to take time off work to be with my children. A great deal of planning and negotiating with my employer needed to be done well in advance.

To enjoy first times, a father needs to be there and to be involved. Joining in your children's numerous activities provides a father with the opportunity to be involved in a first. The activities can be anything from going with them on a day trip at school, to helping them read a book, to driving them different places, to attending a concert with them, to a more planned activity like a family vacation.

THE GEEK MISSED

I t's a family tradition. Early every September, my wife Karen and I take our daughters Alexandra and Ailène to the local fair for a day. It is always a very busy time for the family with many engaging activities to participate in. We always have a lot of fun.

On our trip to the fair when the kids were six and thirteen, lots of children were carrying large plush animals around the midway area throughout the morning. Alexandra, my younger daughter, pointed these out to me and on a number of occasions asked if she would be able to get one of them. She thought I could simply buy one for her. However, I informed her that it would be necessary to win one of the midway games to get one. Alexandra didn't fully comprehend this; she assumed that every time you played the game, you won a prize. Again I tried to describe to her the odds of winning and the whole principle of luck, but I quickly realized it was fruitless.

I asked Alexandra which sort of game she would like to try and eventually she picked one. As Alexandra, Ailène, and I approached the booth, it was apparent that the game she chose was not going to produce a sudden prize. The principle of the game was to throw a baseball at three little wooden pins. One had two chances to knock down all three pins and win a prize. After several prizes, one could trade up for one of the large plush animals that my daughter wanted.

I gave the attendant coupons, and he gave me the baseballs. I handed them to Alexandra; however, she was quite reluctant to throw them and asked if I would do so. On my first throw, I hit two pins, which fell over. On the second throw, I missed. Nothing. The attendant encouraged me to play again. However, I could tell this was going to be an expensive process and decided to stop. As we walked away from the booth, Alexandra started to sob and then cry incredibly loud. She almost reached the point of wailing. Other fair-goers were beginning to notice this distraught child, and Ailène was becoming uncomfortable. I stopped to talk to Alexandra to calm her down, but to no avail. Suddenly, Ailène said, "Keep it down. Can't you see the geek missed?" This comment came from nowhere. It certainly did not help console Alexandra.

Eventually, we found another game where a prize was guaranteed every time. Alexandra participated in that game, won a prize, and immediately cheered up.

For most of her six years, Alexandra had experienced my being with her at all stages of her development. She had idolized me over the years and put me in the position that I could never disappoint her. Suddenly, I had let her down.

Ailène, on the other hand, had reached puberty. She was feeling the need to push me away, a necessary task. There were times when she needed to devalue both me and our relationship as part of the process of forming her own identity.

There at that busy fairground, I had two daughters experiencing two different stages of development, and I was caught in the crossfire. Alexandra still wanted me to be the father who was always there and involved with her, never letting her down. Ailène was feeling the need to begin to separate herself from me and to see me as being human and having flaws.

Ailène, as she has reached adolescence, is beginning to feel the need to flex her own muscles and explore her sense of independence from her parents. It is time to separate herself from me as her father, and she frequently describes how she feels embarrassed when I am around. She often calls me a "loser" in a teasing manner.

One night when I kissed Ailène at bedtime, I noticed that she took her hand and wiped off the side of her face. I asked her what she had done. She said, "the saliva in your mouth has been recycling for forty-eight years and must be acid-like." But as I turned around and left the room, she ran over, gave me a hug and told me she loved me. I could feel the struggle she was experiencing now that she was developing into her own world while continuing to want to engage in a relationship with me. I'm sure that now she has secrets with her friends that she does not tell me, nor should she.

If a dad reaches the point of being over-idealized, then it is quite possible that a male that a daughter meets later on, especially in adolescence, and especially in an intimate relationship, will never match up to the daughter's template of the perfect father.

Over time, as they grow, children move into and out of the mother–father–me triad that begins at birth. A sense of self begins to form. As the world expands to include others such as siblings, relatives, and friends, and children move toward becoming toddlers, a sense of individuality emerges. As they reach latency and then puberty, children begin to expand their network of friends and form new relationships for themselves. This intimacy expands and continues in relationships with others, and we see the closeness an adolescent boyfriend and girlfriend have. Eventually, the intimacy intensifies and the young adult begins to seek out a relationship with a partner, perhaps with a view to one day having children of their own with that person.

As children establish their own personhood, they need an involved, responsible father and mother as a secure base to stand on. Part of being there is knowing when not to be there. It hurts, but sometimes you have to let a child push you away.

Being an involved, responsible father also means that one needs to fall from grace. And that is okay.

The quality of the initial relationship of a father's being there and being involved will have a strong effect on the type of partner the young adult will choose. Your child will look for aspects of the positive nurturing relationship he or she has had with you as father.

PICK YOUR RIDE

My wife Karen and I try to avoid roller coasters and other rides that spin upside-down or move very fast. We do the same with extremely high Ferris wheels that leave a person with the feeling of dangling in mid-air. Karen will simply not get on them. If need be, I am able to tolerate these rides, but I find myself unable to relax and enjoy them as other people are able to do (or appear to be doing). I notice a similar feeling when I watch an IMAX movie that has a great deal of motion throughout it. Often I have to turn my head away or close my eyes.

What I found interesting was how Ailène experienced the same feelings as we did. When she was quite young, we would often select rides at the fair that were rather tame in nature and IMAX films that were similar to travel documentaries. She did not seem to complain and enjoyed this safer approach. As she became older, I encouraged her to go on some faster types of rides and even offered to accompany her. I could, however, sense her reluctance.

As Ailène reached her teen years, she became more willing to try these rides, especially when accompanied by her friends. Even though I had been on some of the rides, I believe she sensed that I was quite tense and unable to enjoy the experience. It was apparent that her friends encouraged her to experience the rides differently, which she found exciting and enjoyable.

As a teenager, Ailène has been able to pass this fun on to her sister. Alexandra, unlike Ailène when she was that age, will go on a number of these rides and boldly want to return and do it all over again. I do not mind participating with her, though I feel there is a limit to my endurance.

It came to a head when we visited Walt Disney World in Florida several years ago. Ailène was an adventuresome twelve-year-old interested in the scarier rides, and Alexandra was more than eager to accompany her. My wife and I, however, weren't so sure about participating in their plans. Even though Ailène and Alexandra were willing to go on some rides together, I still felt that I wanted to join in the experience with them. It would not be much longer before Ailène would prefer the company of her friends over that of her father. Time was running out.

I decided to start out on something that appeared easy to handle and that was the Big Thunder Mountain Railroad roller coaster ride. Boldly, I walked right up to the front of the line with my children. As there were few line-ups at that time of year, we were able to board immediately. This was going to be my first true roller coaster experience. On the other hand, both Ailène and Alexandra were veterans.

The ride took off with a sudden lurch and immediately sped up. Not only were there the usual roller coaster effects, but there was an abruptness to the ride itself. I felt as if I was being thrown about. At the start it was not too difficult to tolerate. As the ride continued, however, I found it to be increasingly anxiety-producing, especially as we went around curves and through dark tunnels. Soon, Alexandra became upset and started to cry. She put her head on my shoulder and hid her eyes with her hands. I found it easier to bend toward her and console her. Therefore, I was able to success-fully avoid the experience of the ride myself. It calmed me down. On the other hand, Ailène was laughing, having fun, and holding up her arms throughout the entire ride. At one point, she screamed out for me to look up. I did so, briefly.

As the ride ended, we started to get off. One of the staff persons said as there was no line-up and very few people were getting on the ride, so we could go around again if we wished. Ailène immediately begged me to stay on with her to try it a second time. Alexandra, on the other hand, had had enough and was eagerly looking for her mother.

As we walked away, I pretended to look calm and cool about the situation. In truth, I felt rattled. Ailène asked me if I had enjoyed myself. She also asked me why I was hiding my head throughout the ride. I tried to cover-up my fear. I said that I was actually concerned about Alexandra and her crying and felt the need to calm her down. Ailène said she had had fun and was looking forward to the next ride, Splash Mountain. That next ride was only a few steps away. I felt that I had reached my limit with Big Thunder Mountain Railroad and was thinking of all possible ways that I could avoid going on Splash Mountain.

As we passed by Splash Mountain, I could sense that even Ailène was hesitant about trying it out. I immediately seized on this feeling and managed somehow to get us all to walk past the ride. I am sure if I had had a little more ambition to go on this ride, both girls would have gone on it. Interestingly, several months later Ailène and her girlfriend went down that very ride, and Ailène brought home a picture to show what fun she had had.

I admit that I am a coward of sorts. Sometimes I have even found it difficult to stand in the subway station as a train rushes along the track toward me. I find myself pulling back and turning toward the wall to look away. The sudden gush of air almost takes the breath out of me. I am not sure what this is about. However, it is clear that over the years we have not exposed our daughters to certain types of rides. In a way, our fears have become theirs. It took Ailène's maturation into adolescence and coaxing from her friends for her to realize that she could have different experiences and reactions from those of her parents.

When I was a child I developed a dislike for certain foods. Some of these dislikes were similar to those of both my mother and my father. However, when I experienced some of these foods as a young man, I thoroughly enjoyed them. It became apparent to me that many of my tastes were in part my parents' tastes.

There are times when your interests become your child's interests, and your fears can be their fears. Your child learns a great deal about the world through you and your partner. Until their horizons broaden with exposure to other individuals in their lives and they begin to formulate their own perceptions, they observe you and adopt your reactions.

As a father, you imprint a great deal upon your child. This is not wrong, but it is important for you to be aware of how your child sees you. The way you cope, react to certain situations, involve yourself with others and solve problems — all these behaviours send your child a message. Your child will start out doing the same. In time, however, children also take in aspects of other people that further contribute to their formulations of a sense of identity for themselves.

I am pleased that Ailène can experience other persons as she grows older and is able to combine their attitudes with mine into a life of her own.

PIANO STYLES

My interest in music came from my mother; my father was not able to carry a tune. He was very self-conscious about singing in public, especially in church, and he had absolutely no interest in piano. At the age of twelve, he once purchased a ukulele and tried to learn how to play it. Eventually, he gave up. That instrument is now in my possession.

My mother enjoyed music, especially piano, and at an early age I was encouraged to take piano lessons along with both of my sisters. The problem was that I really did not like to practice. Even though I was encouraged from time to time by both of my parents, I did not go very far with piano. On occasion, my mother would sit down beside me on the piano bench when I did practice. However, with three children taking piano, helping us with our practicing put a strain on her time. As a teenager, I became interested in playing the guitar and actually went back to taking piano and theory lessons so I could write music.

On one occasion when I was about eleven, my father asked me to play the piano in front of visitors who came to our home. I found it difficult to do this and quickly ran out of the room. After the visitors left, my father expressed his disappointment in my behaviour. I have no explanation as to why I did what I did. I felt very self-conscious about his request. I think this feeling of self-consciousness also extended to singing in a choir in front of others. Even though I enjoyed music and could carry a tune, I felt the same way my father did when put in a position in front of others.

My older daughter, Ailène, started playing the piano at the age of five. She picked up on the technique quickly, and with my persuasion learned how to practice on a regular basis. I realized that if I sat down with her at each practice, especially in the early grades, she would stick with it. Ailène was hesitant about playing in front of others; however, with support, she entered a local piano competition on a yearly basis and played in school concerts. She also completed her theory exams each year. Over time, Ailène took more of the initiative in practicing and my presence was less and less required.

By the time she entered the grade five level in piano, she had passed the point where I was able to read the music with her. I decided to take piano lessons and attempted to keep up with her, but it was difficult to do. Those lessons required practice — and much more of a time commitment than I had intended. I was not able to follow through on the lessons beyond the first year. By then, Ailène had anchored herself in a practice routine and was going on quite well alone. She would occasionally request that I sit down and listen to how she was doing, and I made a point of attending every recital and concert she was involved in.

When Alexandra started taking piano, I assumed her learning style would be very much like that of her older sister. But both Alexandra and I were frustrated from the start and I realized my assumption was wrong. Alexandra had her own way of learning to play the piano, and at the beginning I could not see that. She had her own way of grasping the technique of playing, and I was unsure of what she actually needed to do. Sitting down beside her at each practice was obviously not enough. It was just as important to understand how she was learning. It was necessary for Alexandra to withdraw from piano lessons for awhile. I now realize my error.

I learned a valuable lesson, both from my daughters and from my own experience practicing and playing on the piano, that though the learning process is enhanced by the relationship between the parents and the child and the parents' level of involvement in the activity, the style of involvement is key. On one hand, my mother enjoyed piano and would sit down with me as I started to practice, though it was difficult for her to be consistent. On the other hand, my father did not really enjoy involving himself in any musical activity. He liked music but preferred to sit and listen. He was extremely self-conscious about his musical ability (or lack thereof) and I quickly took this attitude upon myself. I internalized the limitations he placed on himself in terms of his own musical abilities. In this way, I held myself back musically.

Looking back, I realize now the importance of my being involved with both of my daughters' practicing and ways of learning. It was not enough to just sit down with each of them at practice times. I needed to make that concerted effort to be involved with them in their music.

I did manage to check my own attitudes toward music and my self-conscious feelings. I made sure I did not pass these onto my daughters. I was successful in doing this. I did, however, overlook the fact that each of my daughters had her own way of learning, and as Ailène was the oldest, I immediately adopted her style. I unfairly assumed that Alexandra would have the same learning method, but she did not.

This erroneous assumption on my part created stress, especially for Alexandra. I could feel her tension as we both approached the piano. She would do anything to get out of practicing, and on several occasions she wanted to avoid me altogether at these times. What could have been a fun activity had now become a chore for both of us.

Join your children in their interests and activities and have fun with them. Participate in them together. However, also recognize that each child has his or her own learning style, and allow them to take the lead in teaching you how they learn.

YOU'RE EMBARRASSING ME

When my daughters reached about seven or eight years of age, they started informing me that some of my interactions were "icky" and embarrassing. As my oldest daughter Ailène entered the teen years, this feeling began to intensify for her.

The feelings developed progressively. As mentioned earlier, one evening when I went into her room to say good night to her, I leaned over and kissed her on the forehead. As I stood up, I noticed that she quickly wiped away the kiss with her hand, but tried to do it in a way that I would not see it. However, I did notice it. She said that she recently learned in school that the saliva in a person's mouth recycles, and therefore the saliva in mine must be forty-eight years old, and likely acidic. She also concluded that this must have caused my tongue to crack, and that perhaps I should not be kissing her anymore. I am not sure if this was just a way to show more of an emotional individuality, or if she was now viewing me as someone from an older generation who is not really "with it," or both. This reaction that she had to me progressed further, and soon centred on my appearance, the way I presented myself in public, and so on.

Recently Ailène asked me to go to the local mall with her to look at some items of clothing that she was interested in. We drove over to the mall and went inside. As we were walking along, my daughter suddenly darted behind me and ran off in another direction. She rejoined me a few seconds later. I asked her what had happened. She said that she had seen some friends from school approaching us and wanted to avoid them. It was apparent that she didn't want them to see her with me. When I asked her if that was the case, she said, "Yes; sometimes you embarrass me."

I now make concerted attempts to not joke around with Ailène like I used to, especially in public. Even though I have succeeded at this, it appears that my very presence at times is somewhat of an embarrassment to her. Often when I wear clothes that I feel are nice, and that match, Ailène is able to find the slightest variation in shade or style and leave me with the feeling that I am incompetent when it comes to being able to dress myself properly.

Alexandra has entered this phase at an earlier age by imitating her older sister. Often when I drive her to school in the morning, she prefers that I do not kiss her on the cheek. However, I may kiss my hand and she then kisses her hand and we then touch hands. No one sees this. She feels more comfortable and less self-conscious about this. Alexandra is only eight years old and I do not recall Ailène feeling this way at that age.

As they grow, both of my daughters seem to feel not just more self-aware but also more self-conscious. They have increasingly become more aware of their own appearances, as they relate to others'. Their network of relating to others is expanding beyond the family, and they have more friends each year. It is important for each of them to express their own independence and feelings of self-mastery. I believe that an important part of this process is the need to target me and to point out my shortcomings. As they become older, they are clearly drawing a distinctive boundary between my generation and theirs, so I do not feel insulted by their comments toward me; I am, however, surprised at how out of date I have suddenly become!

A child needs to express how different they are from you as father. The child is developing their own ways of relating to others and understanding the world. An integral part of this process is that they feel confident enough in their relationship with you to challenge you. How you react to those challenges is very important. If you are able to tolerate their comments about you and not be confrontational with them, you contribute to their sense of self-mastery and feelings of efficacy. As adolescence approaches, your child feels the need to separate from you and individuate. They do this in part by expressing how they differ from you.

As your child moves toward expressing feelings of being self-conscious, they tend to challenge you more. At times you may feel like you are being picked on. This challenging progresses into a feeling that you are embarrassing them, especially around their friends. Often parents will say that when they take their child to a friend's home or to school, the child may ask to be dropped off a block sooner, so as not to be seen with them.

As a father, you need not feel negative about yourself when you experience these types of interactions with your child. For your child to be able to do this demonstrates that they feel secure in their attachment to you.

HUG FIGHTS

Over the years, my daughters and I have enjoyed wrestling together, whether we wrestled on the bed or on the floor. Sometimes it was quite spontaneous, or was a response to watching a wrestling program on TV. Those programs would make them quite rambunctious. They would announce a fight and insisted on dressing in wrestling attire before we started. They put large work-socks over their hands, pulled on my t-shirts, found a pair of boxer shorts, put on wool caps and — presto — they were ready to do battle. It was quite humorous to look at them wearing these clothes and jumping around in preparation and anticipation of wrestling with father. As soon as the costumes were on, their personas changed and they were ready for the match.

A large blanket on the floor or the bed acted as the wrestling mat. We would crawl onto the blanket and Ailène in particular would signal that she was ready by gritting her teeth. Alexandra had a little bike bell that she would ring to start the round, and soon we would begin rolling around. Sometimes there was a one on one match, and other times they tag-teamed me. Each of them enjoyed my holding them up in the air then putting them down on the mat and laying on top of them. Of course, they would quickly squirm out of my holds.

Alexandra and Ailène worked very hard at trying to pin me to the mat. They often won the matches. Each of us would build up quite a sweat and, on occasion, someone would get a minor scratch or a small injury and start to cry, resulting in a time out being called. Their determination was quite striking; Alexandra in particular was very intense about the situation and would grunt and struggle to get me pinned.

At the end of each match we would hug. This was a given, no matter what. Sometimes while hugging we would wrestle, or vice versa. Somehow, we started calling these matches hug fights — a suitable name for what was a rough and tumble situation, yet at the same time, an intimate activity.

I have noticed that most of my physical interactions with my daughters have been those where they are forever tickling me, poking at me, or pinching me. They also liked, when they were younger, to hold my hand when we were walking down the street. They constantly wanted to play with me, to roughhouse, especially when we were at home.

Their style of interacting with me is different than their style with their mother. Research has confirmed that this is often the case. Usually a mother and child have more of a homeostatic relationship, an intimate coming together in a quiet manner. This could mean sitting on the couch reading a book, singing, or whatever. Fathers, on the other hand, demonstrate a more disruptive manner; children view fathers as objects to be involved with playfully and physically. With each of my daughters, as much as there is this physical hands-on interaction that occurs, it builds into an intimate hug.

To a child, the father does not simply supply the toy, he is the toy. Your child enjoys jumping up and down on you or generally just playing with you. I believe this is the way the child learns about you as a dad and has fun doing it. As the toy, your child engages with you in a special way. A man has his way to play and to be involved with a child that is different from a woman's. Your child senses this.

There are many other things that a father does differently with his baby and child. He picks them up differently, holds them differently, and involves himself differently than a mother does. The two styles of father and mother are complementary in a child's development, and both are very important. Through these interactions, a child learns different ways of relating with others in the outside world.

My daughters chose the right term. "Hug fight" is the perfect description of this unique combination of aggressiveness and intimacy.

WATCHING FROM A DISTANCE

The summer before Ailène entered high school, she was thirteen years old and very excited about the upcoming new experience. She also wanted to try out for the grade nine girls' basketball team. She knew that basketball was something that she could excel at. It had all started when she was five years of age, and I put up a basketball net in the driveway. I spent time playing with her, and she was able to develop a sense of self-mastery and confidence the more she played the sport. I notice now that my younger daughter, Alexandra, is doing the same.

In preparing for the high school tryouts, my daughter attended local basketball camps throughout the summer.

She was also quite interested in attending one offered by the Detroit Pistons in Michigan. She was anxious prior to us leaving for Detroit, as she felt that there would be other campers her age that would play much better than she could. She was concerned that she was not good enough. I said that this was not the case, and that these were players who wanted to learn how to further develop their basketball skills, just like she did. I also added that she had been playing league basketball for a number of years, had attended numerous other camps, and that she had developed some very good skills of her own.

As we drove to the camp, another concern arose. Ailène felt that she would not know anyone and would find it difficult to meet new friends. As I spoke to her about this, it became apparent that this was also the feeling that she was having regarding attending high school in September.

Throughout her week at the camp, Ailène quickly met other girls her age with whom she became friends. She enjoyed being there and actively participated in all levels of the camp program.

Karen, Alexandra, and I stayed at a nearby motel. Parents were invited to watch the camp throughout the day, and I chose to sit in the stands on several afternoons. I watched Ailène go through a number of different drills and play several games. While sitting there, I also worked on the outline of this book as well as its content. Occasionally I would glance down at my daughter and watch her, as her team rotated from station to station. I was quite proud of how she was engaging with the other campers, while at the same time developing her basketball skills.

I also noticed that Ailène glanced toward me from time to time. This was a rather large stadium, and there were not very many parents there. It was easy to get lost in the number of empty chairs surrounding each of us. However, Ailène quickly noticed where I was sitting. Each time she glanced at me she would smile, then go back to playing basketball.

During the break, Ailène climbed up the stairs to see me. She brought with her a sports-drink that I was to sample and critique. She stood there briefly and talked, then went back courtside to continue playing with the other campers.

Although Ailène and the other girls were going through routine drills, I enjoyed being there that afternoon to watch. To see this person who was once a baby that I had held in my arms, had watched learn to walk, had seen move away from me to participate in activities with other kids, now standing out there even more on her own, exhibiting her independence . . . well, you parents get the picture. I was touched that she still felt she needed the reassurance; the security that I was still there in her life.

She wanted to be independent, yet she needed to feel the security that I was nearby.

A father assists in setting the stage for that feeling of being special and important. Your involvement contributes to your child's feelings of self-worth and self-esteem. You help in establishing a secure base for your child to stand on.

Research has shown that the involvement of a father in their lives helps contribute to teen girls' feelings of confidence, competence, and especially the ability to compete with others. Likewise, research has pointed out that involved fathers help teenage boys to modulate their aggression and to channel it in a respectful, productive manner. A father also contributes to his son's feelings of self-worth and self-esteem as he enters manhood.

My attendance at Ailène's basketball camp was important in contributing to her maturing into adolescence. It was only one small thing but it still mattered a great deal to her. Even though she was only acknowledging me in her quick, glancing manner, she did not feel the need to hide behind me anymore.

After she talked to me in the stands, she returned to her new friends. I could feel myself receding once again into the background. My daughter wanted me there, but she also wanted to be on her own.

The relationship with your child is like a wave against the shoreline. It comes in, washes up on the shore, and then recedes. This is all part of the rhythm of the security of the attachment in the relationship with your child. The more able you are to establish a secure base, the better able your child will be to move toward you and then out into the world.

WE NEED EACH OTHER

In the last week of August of each year, our family rents a cottage on a large lake about a two-hour drive from our home. The cottage is actually a lovely two-storey home located along the waterfront with a beautiful sandy beach just a few metres away. It has a beautiful panoramic view of the water.

Three families, all related, own this home, and several times each year these families come together for special occasions. The centrepiece of this home is a large dining table. There are numerous children in the families, so situated around the table are fourteen chairs, with room for several more. For a stranger visiting the home, the size of the table and the number of chairs is quite striking.

One evening during our traditional vacation at the cottage, I was sitting at this table reading. Ailène came over to me and asked me if I had brought the camera. She asked if I would take a picture of her and her sister sitting at the end of this large table, as I had done in other years. This picture has become a tradition when we visit the cottage. Over the years, I have asked my daughters to sit or stand at the end of the table, and I would go to the other end and take a photograph of them. I told Ailène that yes, I had brought the camera and that we would take a picture. They excitedly got into place at the table.

After returning from the cottage, I decided to look at all the photographs that had been taken at that table over the years. I organized them chronologically from when we first started going there as a family. It was interesting to see how my children and family had grown and changed. Some of the earlier photographs are of only one daughter sitting in a high chair, soon to be joined by her sister sitting on her lap. The more recent photos show two rather tall girls standing with their arms around each other, smiling.

Each year, going to this cottage is an event that my family looks forward to. For most families, and especially mine, this opportunity to remove oneself for a week from the daily grind and have time out as a family together is very important. Rules are relaxed, and it is time to have fun. Each year when we return to the cottage, I find it hard to believe how fast the previous year has passed by. Likewise, after we have been there for a week, I am startled by how quickly time at the cottage has gone by.

While we are at the cottage, I often find myself recalling various memories from prior visits, and I feel a sense of pride in my family. The cottage is like a time out in a game. The opportunity is made to review, refresh, and reflect on the past year before we start out on the year about to come.

The living memories you have read about in this book have several common threads. These threads weave a tapestry showing the importance of an involved, responsible father in a child's life. As an involved, responsible father, you have an essential role in your child's development. With your involvement and responsibility, you form a nurturing attachment with your child that is extremely important in contributing to how they develop as a person. The relationship formed between you and your child is very special.

The quality of your involvement in what will become a surprisingly short time in your child's life is entirely up to you and how well you understand your history, yourself, your child, and your partner. To follow your own style, to meet your child at their level, and to enjoy all stages of your child's development are all ingredients of the quality of attachment you form with your child.

Being there is what it is all about. Your relationship with your child is similar to establishing an investment certificate at the bank, which you "lock in" over a period of time. Just as you cannot tell right away how your investment will do, you are not able, in the short term, to tell how good a father you actually are. However, over time you will reflect back and recall the growth and development of your child. You will see how your investment in your child's life has matured.

The true value of this certificate becomes apparent when you notice the quality of attachments your child has with other people and their ability to form their own nurturing relationships.

A father needs a child, just as a child needs a father. We need each other.

You as a father are very important in your child's life. Be there, be involved, be responsible.

Dads can do it!

AFTERWORD

As my own experiences in this book make clear, "father" is a verb, not a noun. Fathering is an activity for life. Fathers change as they and their children age. Experiences with their own fathers inform their fathering abilities. In fact, the seeds of fatherhood are first sown in the child. As the seeds germinate and the quality of the relationship between father and child begins to grow, living memories are created.

As they mature into adulthood, children need to find a way to challenge the authority of their fathers while not destroying the all-important relationship between them. We all need to "freeze the pyjamas;" to communicate with our fathers through symbolic actions such as playing pranks on them, working with them, asking them to share with us the stories of their own fathers and their own childhoods. In that way, we are affirming our own selfhood, while at the same time joining in play together.

This ever shifting process of coming together and growing apart is the dance of the relationship between a father and his child. Now more than ever, our society needs a generation of men who are willing to enter into this dance and embrace their ability to nurture the next generation. After all, one major measure of ourselves as a society is how we encourage involved, responsible fatherhood.

Fathers, enjoy the responsibility, joy, and gift of being a father!

APPENDIX:

10 + 1 TIPS
TO BE AN INVOLVED FATHER

1. **Support and respect the mother of your children.**
   By both the mother and the father showing respect for each other, children grow up in a secure, nurturing environment. Strengthen your relationship as a couple by keeping channels of communication and romance open. Children learn from this openness and gain respect for themselves and others through it.

2. **Work together as a team, sharing equally in all child-rearing tasks.**
   Get up at night to help look after your child. Take

an active role in supportive fathering of the breast-fed baby if your child is a newborn. Discuss concerns and issues you have about your child's health, safety, and development with your partner. Realize that your partnership means a father's active involvement as well as mother's.

3. **Spend time with your children.**
Read to your child. Play with him or her. Attend your child's school events, music recitals, and sporting events. Participate in the school classroom, or assist with a field trip. Do an organized activity together, such as hockey or gymnastics. Have fun together doing chores around the home, and let your child help out in his or her own way. Also, just spend some quiet time together. Children want your involvement in their lives and need you to help them develop their sense of self-confidence. Putting your children first may mean reprioritizing your life. The rewards are great and will last a lifetime for both you and your child.

4. **Show love and affection toward your child.**
Be committed to your child's emotional well-being. Encourage and teach your child to live a life

of intimacy and integrity with respect for others. Reward your child's desirable behaviour, and be prepared to offer guidance for less positive behaviour. Establishing boundaries, setting reasonable limits, and disciplining in a fair manner might be necessary on occasion. Children need to understand how their behaviour may affect others. This understanding is reflected in a secure, loving, and caring relationship with you.

5.   **Protect your family.**
Enjoy the physical maturation of your child and be aware of your child's immunization record and visits to the family doctor or dentist. Your child's health is as much your responsibility as it is the mother's. If necessary, childproof the home environment, securing items that are potentially dangerous to the child. Teach "street-smarts," and how your child can learn to take care of him- or herself if necessary. Educate your child about the world outside the home so that he or she is prepared.

6.   **Spend time together as a family.**
Share a meal together on a daily basis. While eating, listen to your children and encourage them to talk about their day. Provide them with support

and advice on how to cope with the various situations they experience. You may also want to consider visiting friends and relatives as a family. Go bowling, swimming, skating, fishing, etc. together. Attend a community event. Ask your children to help plan a family vacation and let them assist you in organizing it. Help your children develop good judgment relative to the TV by letting them help to choose a video or TV show, and watch it together. Ideas for family activities are numerous and help a child experience fun with a sense of warmth and security. These feelings will enrich your child's life as he or she grows.

7.   **Tell your story.**

The history of your parents and your own family can be interesting to your child. A child often feels that the world began at his or her birth. Through your reflections on your past, you provide your child with an intriguing sense of history and of past generations. You need not tell them all the details of your history, only those that leave your child with the feeling that you too were once a child and you grew up and became an involved father.

8. **Promote and encourage your place of work to be father-friendly.**

   Organize a Father's Day event with your colleagues such as a dads' picnic. Have photographs of your family displayed at work, and take along pictures your children have made. If possible, promote a "bring your child to work" day. Schedule time in your day-planner to be at home with your child doing homework, attending school, or seeing a movie together. Educate your children about your work environment, and tell them the importance of work to you. They will better understand when they see that you are working for them, and to meet the needs of your family.

9. **Set an example.**

   Be a model to your child for manners, honesty, and self-discipline. Earn the right to be listened to by your children. Remember, your child is watching you and your interactions with others. By setting a nurturing example, you can promote a feeling of acceptance and respect in your own child.

10. **Being an involved father is for life.**

    Your children will grow up and perhaps eventually will have children of their own. Your participation in their lives and those of their children is ongoing. Fatherhood is a lifelong commitment and your relationship with your child is forever.

10+1. Dads can do it!

Believe in yourself, and in your potential to be an active, caring father. Every child deserves a loving, involved father.

CPSIA information can be obtained
at www.ICGtesting.com
Printed in the USA
LVOW03s0954271217
560894LV00011B/105/P